Polish Air Force
Fighter Aircraft, 1940-1942

Polish Air Force Fighter Aircraft, 1940–1942

From the Battle of France to the Dieppe Raid

Peter Sikora

AIR WORLD

First published in Great Britain in 2023 by
Pen & Sword Air World
An imprint of Pen & Sword Books Limited
Yorkshire – Philadelphia

ISBN 978 1 39905 102 6

Typeset by Mac Style
Printed in the UK by CPI Group (UK) Ltd, Croydon, CR0 4YY.

Pen & Sword Books Limited incorporates the imprints of After the Battle,
Atlas, Archaeology, Aviation, Discovery, Family History, Fiction, History,
Maritime, Military, Military Classics, Politics, Select, Transport, True Crime,
Air World, Frontline Publishing, Leo Cooper, Remember When, Seaforth
Publishing, The Praetorian Press, Wharncliffe Local History, Wharncliffe
Transport, Wharncliffe True Crime and White Owl.

For a complete list of Pen & Sword titles please contact

PEN & SWORD BOOKS LIMITED
47 Church Street, Barnsley, South Yorkshire, S70 2AS, England
E-mail: enquiries@pen-and-sword.co.uk
Website: www.pen-and-sword.co.uk
or
PEN AND SWORD BOOKS
1950 Lawrence Rd, Havertown, PA 19083, USA
E-mail: uspen-and-sword@casematepublishers.com
Website: www.penandswordbooks.com

Contents

Introduction

*'The Polish Fighter Pilot is imbued with the determination to exterminate Germans –
All his energies are absorbed in this purpose. "The only good German is a dead German".
"Do not shoot only into their engines – some may come down alive and go back to Germany
after the war." (…) Their pride is without vanity. Their gallantry is "not for the sake of
a ribboned coat". (…) Polish pride includes such attributes as courage, honour, patriotism
(and its younger brother, esprit de corps), self-respect, good manners, skill, determination
and, at the lower end of the scale, obstinacy. (…) In any event, there are no fellows more
admirable than the Polish fighter pilots.'*
Gp Cpt Theodore McEvoy, RAF Northolt Station Commander[1].

Some may say that to deserve such kind words and compliments, Polish fighter pilots had to fight very hard from the early hours of the Second World War, gaining their experience and baptism of fire. In fact, however, the fight for freedom accompanied the newly born Polish Air Service/Polish Military Aviation since its beginning in November 1918 during the wars with Ukraine and Bolshevik Russia, when the first fighter units were employed to secure unsteady borders and to prevent intruders from taking what was just earned. To be even more precise, we would need to go back to the First World War, in which the Polish fliers, men with no country yet, were conscripted into occupant armies of the Empires of Austro – Hungary, Germany and Russia. This was actually the time, specifically 1915, when Flik 27's flier Roman Florer[2] claimed an aerial victory over an Italian aircraft after shooting at it with a handgun! It was not an isolated incident though, his fellow countryman Antoni Mroczkowski, at that time fighting on the opposite side, and representing the Tsar's forces, claimed an Austrian biplane using the same method. Poles were undoubtedly among the aerial war pioneers!

Between 1918, when reborn, and 1939 when Poland fought her lonely defensive war that sealed the fate of Polish people, the country had developed a range of more or less successful, domestically designed and built, fighter aircraft, with the most famous lane of technically advanced PZL single seaters fitted with the seagull shaped wings. Despite being the world's first metal fighters in the mid-1930s, ahead of the competitors, in September 1939, Polish fighter pilots were already disadvantaged, poorly equipped and outnumbered. In the face of a new air power, never seen before, being brave, aggressive, trenchant and well trained had not prevented their honourable and inevitable failure. To continue their fight in the hope of returning their bellowed homeland to its rightful owners, over 12,000 airmen from Poland[3] (including a significant number of fighter pilots) started their journey westwards via Rumania, Hungary, Yugoslavia, Greece, Italy or via Baltic countries.

After the severe winter of 1939/1940 and a period of French apathy, finally in the early spring of 1940 initial training started and the Polish fighter pilots were posted to Lyon-Bron, where initially a Training Squadron and later a (Polish) Air Force Training Centre were formed. There were other locations too, including Toulouse, Montpellier, Avord, Etampes, Tours, Mions and a few others. Primarily it was decided to form three totally Polish manned fighter units known as: I Fighter Squadron to be led by Lt.Col. Leopold Pamuła, II Fighter Squadron 'Cracow – Poznań' under the command of Maj. Mieczysław Mümler and III Fighter Squadron 'Dęblin' of Maj. Józef Kępiński. I Fighter Squadron ended as a 'paper project' only, and its pilots were divided into small sections soon to be attached to numerous units of Armée de l'Air, including Défense Aérienne du Territorie (Territorial Air Defence). II Fighter Squadron eventually evolved into the so called 'Montpellier Flight' or 'Montpellier Group', and after completion of training, small Polish fighter sections were posted to various French frontline squadrons. III Fighter Squadron was supposed to be sent to Finland to fight against the Soviets, hence it received its unofficial name 'The Finish Squadron'. Unfortunately during an extensive training that the Poles undertook, the armistice was signed between USSR and Finland, therefore the name and designation for the Polish formation was no longer needed and it was changed to Groupe de Chasse 1/145 'Varsovie' (Warsaw). During the spring of 1940 GC 1/145 participated in the Battle of France as the only Polish fighter squadron. During the French Campaign, which only lasted a few days longer than the defence of Poland, Polish fighters, flying mainly Morane Saulnier MS.406s, Marcel Bloch MB.151s and MB152s, Caudron Renault CR. 714 Cyclones but also Curtiss H.75A Hawks, Kolhooven FK.58s, Arsenal VG-33s, Dewoitine D.501s, D.510s and D.520s, as well as Nieuport Delage NiD.622s, lost nine of their pilots in combat, four in flying accidents and a further three due to other circumstances. All these for the prize of 56 enemy aircraft destroyed in combat by the Poles[4] and a further six damaged.[5]

While in France[6], it was agreed that two light bomber squadrons would be formed in Britain in parallel from the Polish personnel. To arrange the flying crews for both, the fighter pilots were chosen as well as their bomber colleagues. The quality and ability of either group, who lost one campaign already, hence in British eyes of questionable value, were naturally disputable at this early stage. This was followed by the lack of Polish personnel speaking the English language, undoubtedly crucial to operate when under command of the RAF[7]. Luckily in the spring of 1940 the Royal Air Force and Fighter Command's main man ACM Hugh 'Stuffy' Dowding softened, being also cornered by the stormy waves of the upcoming events, and the training on Hurricanes and Spitfires began.

The first Poles were posted to Fighter Command squadrons and Flg Off Antoni Ostowicz of No. 145 Squadron flew the first operational sortie[8], while a decision was made to form two Polish units too: Nos. 302 (13 July) and 303 (2 August). Ostowicz's victory[9] marked the official beginning of the Polish participation in the Battle of

Britain[10] (despite what various sources claim), at the very beginning of the Battle![11] This also gave foundation for a long lasting cooperation between the re-born and re-grouped fighter forces from Poland and their Allied brothers in arms, giving a clear way to their achievements and valuable input into the war effort.

Following the Polish successes, the green light was switched on and further squadrons were formed: 306 and 308 being day fighter units, and 307 a night fighter. Neither took part in the Battle of Britain did not see action until December 1940, except No. 306 Sqn which flew its first operational sortie on 29 October 1940. Nos. 315, 316 and 317 Squadrons were formed between 21 January and 23 February, 1941. In addition No. 318 Fighter Reconnaissance Squadron was created in March 1943, and finally No. 309 (originally formed in October of 1940 as Army Co-operation) was transferred to Fighter Command in June of 1943. During their five years of operational service, the Polish Air Force fighter squadrons used a wide variety of aircraft. These included Hawker Hurricane Is, IIs and IVs, Supermarine Spitfire Is, IIs, Vs, IXs and XVIs, North American Mustang Is, IIIs and IVs, Boulton Paul Defiants, Bristol Beaufighter IIFs, VIFs and de Havilland Mosquito NF.IIs, FB.VIs, XIIs, XIIIs and NFXXXs.

Following the initial need of their improvement of the English language as well as familiarisation with the aerial tactics implemented by the RAF, over 70 Polish fliers were a part of British squadrons during the Battle of Britain. This practice continued later and many of them gained their first flying experience in day and night fighter RAF units during few following years. In other cases the Polish fighter pilots, with combat experience already achieved among their countrymen, were moved to non-Polish units too, to pass on aerial experience and to strengthen the bond between Polish and RAF airmen! Thanks to an exchange agreement with the Allies, the Poles also had a chance to fly the types of aircraft never used by the exiled Polish Air Force squadrons such as Hawker Tempest, Hawker Typhoon, Curtiss P-40 Kittyhawk or Douglas Havoc. This tendency was descending over the years with the men gaining required knowledge and skills, but also with fewer new pilots to train, which was the effect of supply drying up.

The first aerial victory claimed by a Pole in a non-Polish unit after the Battle of Britain was reported on 11 November 1940 by Sgt Michał Maciejowski of 249 Sqn RAF (1 Bf 109) and the last kill was noted on 4 July 1944 by Flt Lt Michał Kolubiński from 66 Sqn RAF (also Bf 109), with the total score of over 24 enemy aircraft destroyed across RAF squadrons. A significant number of Polish pilots were posted to USAAF squadrons too, where they were flying P-47 Thunderbolts and P-51 Mustangs.

Bearing in mind the initial British lack of trust, some Poles did rather well on foreign soil, or to be precise, under foreign skies, by gaining command of RAF Squadrons. These men were: Sqn Ldrs Jerzy Jankiewicz (No. 222 Sqn), Stanisław Skalski (No. 601 Sqn), Eugeniusz Horbaczewski (No. 43 Sqn). Others led much larger Allied units: Wg Cdr Jan Zumbach (No. 135 Wing), Gp Cpts Tadeusz Rolski, Aleksander Gabszewicz and Stefan Witorzeńć (exclusive command of RAF Stations[12]). Moreover Gp Cpt Aleksander Gabszewicz commanded (No. 18 (Polish) Sector of the 2nd TAF, which consisted of nine squadrons including two British, one Belgian and one New Zealand). Besides receiving the highest Polish military decorations such as the Virtuti Militari Cross and Cross of Valour, numerous fighter pilots of the PAF were awarded by the Allies in recognition of their values and courage. Despite being a rather a sour prize for the much higher price that was paid by blood and tears, for already spilt milk and mainly because all these shiny medals would not return their forever-lost homeland[13] for which Poles tirelessly fought for, it would be right to mention that the Poles undoubtedly deserved the following: Commander, Order of the British Empire presented to three high ranking Polish fighter pilots, whilst three others received an Officer, Order of the British Empire. These were followed by one Member, Order of the British Empire, one Distinguished Service Order and Bar, four Distinguished Service Orders, one Distinguished Flying Cross with two Bars and one Distinguished Flying Cross with one Bar. Many were the recipients of the Distinguished Flying Cross, others the Air Force Cross, Distinguished Flying Medal, Air Force Medal and Military Cross. The British were not the only nation to show their appreciation: American Distinguished Flying Crosses and Silver Stars were pinned onto some of the Poles' tunics, these were men who fought alongside the USAAF squadrons. Many Poles received the French Croix de Guerre for participation in 1940s defence. The Dutch were grateful too, awarding Polish fighters with the Commandeur in de Orde van Oranje-Nassau and Vliegerkruis. Six pilots of No. 318 Squadron were decorated with the Croce al valor militare for participation in the Italian Campaign. And 55 Polish fighter pilots gained an ace title, with some of them coming to Britain with impressive scores from Poland and France.

Since the Battle of Britain the Polish Air Force squadrons[14], as well as individual Polish pilots posted to Allied units, participated in all main Second World War aerial operations including non-stop offensive in 1941, protecting convoys, defending Exeter and Merseyside, 'Jubilee' (Dieppe Raid), Battle of Atlantic, D-Day and following battles over Western Europe, including Battle of Normandy, invasion of Germany, fighting against V1 flying bombs ('Anti-Diver') as well as in the Italian and Tunisian Campaigns. There were Polish crews operating over Malta and one fighter pilot fighting in China against Japanese forces[15]. Ten totally Polish manned fighter squadrons were formed, three fighter wings (1st Polish Wing[16], later No. 131 Airfield / Wing of 2nd TAF; 2nd Polish Wing[17], later No. 133 Airfield / Wing of 2nd TAF and 3rd Polish Wing), but also flying schools including Polish Fighter School[18]. When it became possible to leave the Soviet gulags in 1941, many previously captured airmen were able to evacuate from the frosty and deadly USSR, and travel to England to refresh their skills and to join their colleagues. At the same time many other young men, who barely survived Russian brutality and Siberian winters, as well as volunteers of Polish roots from America, began their experience with aviation by commencing an initial and then fighter training in Britain and refilled PAF squadrons. In all these cases it was an important, yet limited, injection of fresh strength and manpower.

During the hopeless Polish Campaign of 1939, defending fighter forces eliminated 126 enemy aircraft[19] in the air (out of at least 229 lost by Luftwaffe in Poland). Fighter pilots and fighter crews from Poland, while operating under British command, claimed the destruction of over 746 enemy aeroplanes, a further 175 probably destroyed and over 237 damaged, as well as over 190 flying bombs V1 destroyed while on their way to England. There were also strafing (dive attack) missions regularly flown, when ground targets such as airfields, factories supporting the enemy war effort, railways with trains carrying war material, but also marshalling yards, enemy ships, military columns, trucks and armoured vehicles were attacked and often destroyed. All these with the duration of 73,524 operational sorties flown, with the total number of flying hours of 122, 816 and with the loss of 421 airmen killed, 52 missing and 73 captured[20]. These numbers include 224 men killed in action[21]. All these figures do not include thousands of Polish ex-service, men and women, disappointed with the results of the Second World War ending and having no home to return to… It was a heart breaking epilogue for the soldiers, who were the first to fight, to hit and to defend, who were present in the Second World War skies since Sub. Lt. Władysław Gnyś's first kill in the early hours of 1 September 1939.[22]

This book provides an insight into the various types of a military aircraft flown in combat by the Polish fighters since the Battle of France until the disastrous, yet glorious from the PAF perspective, Dieppe Raid in August 1942. Perhaps the limited number of Battle of Britain images used in this book will raise some questions, especially among British readers. The author, inspired by the same Publisher, has previously written two books covering the Polish participation in defending the British Isles in the summer of 1940, therefore the Battle of Britain only has a passing mention in this volume. The selection of over 250 specifically chosen photos describes the Polish journey to the Island of Last Hopes, beginning with the fall of Poland, the Battle of France, the conversion to British aircraft, organisation of Polish units, men, and the major operations in which Polish fighter squadrons were engaged between 1940 and 1942. It is true, though, that even all these photos and the detailed information provided for this material cannot tell the whole story. The human cost especially cannot be fully told throughout these pages. But what is history without trying to say as much as possible? I hope that this book at least answers some of the questions, reveals some of the lesser-known facts and intrigues the reader to learn more. It would be right time to announce that the next instalment *The Polish Air Force Fighter Aircraft 1943-1945. On the Offensive, D-Day to Victory in Europe* will be coming soon.

Opposite: Regaining independence, after 123 years of not existing as a country, was not an easy task. Even before freedom was proclaimed, the war with the neighbouring state of Ukraine began. This was soon followed by Bolshevik Russian aggression. Poland's just formed Air Service had to use all that was available after the First World War left Polish territory plundered. Whether it was a former oppressor's aircraft taken forcibly or scavenged, but also aeroplanes purchased in defeated Germany or Austria; as long as these could fly it did not matter. Here is Sgt Franciszek Jach, a pilot of 1st 'Greater Poland' Squadron photographed in Albatros D. III with the checkerboard, a symbol of Polish Military Aviation, applied upside down, hence against the order issued on 1 December 1918. The pilot claimed a Ukrainian balloon on 9 May 1919, however he was brought down in Albatros No. 3119/17 and captured.

Chapter 1
Per Ardua Ad Astra – Against All Odds

The first fifteen SPAD VIICs of the French Spa 162 Escadrille arrived in Poland with General Józef Haller's Army. These were followed by 22 machines (both VIIC1 and XIIIC1) from the American 138 Aero Squadron. There were also other SPADs purchased from the Americans, including SPAD XIIIC1 no. S7838 (Polish number 24.21) from 17th Aero Squadron (according to some sources from 18th Fighter Squadron) pictured here. In 1920 the Poles bought a further 15 SPAD VIIs and SPAD XIIIs.

Polish production (manufactured by Plage and Laśkiewicz Aircraft Company) under Italian licence Ansaldo A.1 Ballilla no. 1 is pictured in 1923 while at Mokotów aerodrome. This mount was flown by 7th 'Kościuszko' Fighter Squadron's commander, Captain Teofil Dziama, hence tricolour (blue, white and red) stipes across the fuselage and close to the Kościuszko badge. Two years later the unit was renamed as 121st Fighter Squadron and in 1928 as 111th Fighter Squadron. All these were the predecessors of the famous No. 303 Squadron.

PWS-10 was the first military aircraft of Polish design that went into 'mass' production. In fact, only 80 of these aeroplanes were made between 1931 and 1932, and after a rather short stay in fighter squadrons, these were replaced and used for training. Twenty of these fighters we sold to Spain, where they we called 'Chiquita'. A section of PWS-10s from 4th Air Regiment in Toruń was photographed after the new badges were introduced. In 1928, 116th Fighter Squadron was renamed as 142nd Fighter Squadron and instead of two horizontal red slim rectangles on a white square background with a red outline, two flying red ducks with green wings against the background of a white pentagon were accepted as the new emblem. The application was gradual, hence only machine no. 14 is in full colours. Before the war once more this badge (as many others across the regiments) was modified and only one flying duck was introduced. This motif was later incorporated into No. 306 'City of Toruń' Squadron's badge in Britain.

Cpt.Bolesław Orliński, an experienced test pilot, poses in front of PZL P.24/II at Tatoi aerodrome near Athens, Greece, during his promotional tour throughout the Balkans in January 1936. This was to present this aircraft to potential buyers. Note civilian SP-ATO markings partially obscured by the pilot, as the PZL factory owned it. The lack of wheel spats is noteworthy too. This aircraft is fitted with two Vickers 7,92 mm machine guns on both sides of the fuselage and two Oerlikon type F, 20 mm underwing cannons. Orliński also flew the first prototype of this aircraft earlier in May 1933. Eventually PZL P.24s were purchased by Turkey (P.24A and C types), alongside a licence to build these aircraft; Bulgaria also ordered P.24Bs as well as Rumania (P.24Es). Furthermore the latter country built these machines under licence as IAR P-24Es. Another air force using this aircraft was Greece's Royal Hellenic Air Force (P.24F, H and G with 35 mm bulletproof glass of the Perspex-made canopy). Despite unjust 'Cinderella' status, Polish Military Aviation developed a modern aircraft, which, equipped with 20 mm cannons, was ahead of any European fighter aircraft at that time. It was considered by the British Air Ministry as Fairey Fury's replacement, but most probably seemed too foreign for the RAF. Moreover, the British only installed the cannons into mass production on Spitfires in 1941! Bolesław Orliński was also famous for his Warsaw – Tokyo – Warsaw flight in 1926. Years later, in Britain, he was one of the first Poles to try Hurricanes and Spitfires in the air. He also commanded No. 305 'Greater Poland' Squadron flying Mosquitoes.

PZL P.24, which outperformed British Supermarine Type 224 (with the latter being Spitfire's predecessor), would look handsome with RAF roundels. Instead it was exported to Balkan countries, such as Bulgaria, Rumania, Greece and Turkey (where they were flown side by side by Spitfire L1066, that was initially shipped to Poland) and in 1939 not even one aircraft of this type (despite being already outdated, yet still much better than PZL P.11 and PZL P.7) had been used to defend the country of its origin. Only Royal Hellenic Air Force's PZL P.24s fought against the Reggia Aeronautica and Luftwaffe. Picture shows PZL P.24B version demonstrated to Bulgarians at Okęcie aerodrome in October 1937. Note a sliding canopy and four machine guns. B version was also designed to carry four 12.5 kg bombs.

All fighter aircraft used by the Polish Military Aviation during the German invasion were painted in the typical way: Polish khaki (three slightly different types of this colour known as early, medium and late) for the fuselage and upper surfaces and light blue grey or dark blue grey for underwing. PZL P.11c, pictured here, for many years remained quite puzzling, with its 'German style' camouflage of sharp edges. Aircraft no. 3, serial no. 8.138, with underwing non-operational code 62-W, was previously tested with two other P.11s at the Aviation Technical Institute in Warsaw (hence code; where the new form of two tone khaki/olive green camouflage was experimented with), and attached to Pursuit Brigade as a replacement machine. Who flew its final sortie and where this picture was taken still causes discussion (some historians believe to be Cpl. Antoni Joda of 152nd Fighter Squadron/Pursuit Brigade who landed near Zegrze on 9 September 1939 due to engine trouble). It is known, however, that at the last stage, what was of left of no. 3 was transported to Pułtusk. The photo was staged for a more 'dramatic look' by the Germans, as initially this P.11c was found on its back; hence it is believed that the aircraft overturned upon landing.

PZL P.7a no. 6 from 151st Fighter Squadron literally 'captured' by the Germans. This aircraft was flown by Sub.Lt. Zygmunt Kinel on 11 September 1939, when it was hit by ground fire and landed near Zambrów. Although badly wounded, Kinel managed to evade captivity by landing close to the Polish lines (only to be killed on 8 May 1941 while in No. 302 'City of Poznań' Squadron in Britain), but soon after his aircraft played a 'captive' role for this staged photo with two Panzerkampfwagen IIIE tanks from Panzer Regiment 7. Note 151st Squadron's badge of flying blue condor against white cross that was later adopted by No. 317 'City of Wilno' Squadron in Britain.

One of PZL P.11f fighters, of which 95 were built under licence by Romanian I.A.R. in Braşov and photographed at Bucharest Pipera aerodrome. Note Polish type of skis designed by Jerzy Płoszajski in Włodzimierz Szomański workshop. Szomański's brand also monopolised the Polish military market of 1930s by supplying majority of domestic aircraft, including PZL P.7 and P.11, with good quality airscrews designed by Jerzy Bukowski. It was one of the aircraft missing from the skies over Poland in September 1939.

Captured PZL P.7a with Luftwaffe markings that was used for flying training. These types of aircraft were found mostly in the Dęblin area and later repaired.

Chapter 2

Battle of France

Dewoitine D.501s and D.510s (the latter type is seen here) were already obsolete in 1940 and yet were assigned for the numerous Polish training flying schools. Later, due to lack of alternative fighters, these were also used by a few Polish fighter sections to fly patrols. Fortunately no German aeroplanes were encountered.

Sub. Lt. Tadeusz Hojden in the cockpit of Dewoitine D. 501 at Clermont-Ferrand in June 1940. The pilot flew with the Sub. Lt. Antoni Kolubiński's Section DAT, defending Rennes. The pilots complained about the poor state of their aircraft.

Caudron C. 635 Simoun was an aircraft the Poles used for initial familiarisation at Lyon-Bron, Montpellier and a few other bases. The C. 635 photographed here is surrounded by Polish personnel at Lyon-Bron in February 1940.

The other types of aircraft used by the Polish fighter pilots for training were Loire Lo-45 and Loire Lo-46. The aeroplane of the later type no. 33, white 13, underwing no. N-151, is pictured here at Châteauroux aerodrome with an unknown Polish pilot.

Morane Saulnier MS. 406 surrounded by the Polish and French pilots at Etampes, where the Poles, led by Cpt. Walerian Jasionowski, between March and May 1940, participated in a fighter course flying various types of aircraft.

Curtiss Hawk H-75s were used operationally by two Polish DAT Sections led by Cpt. Bronisław Kosiński and Maj. Zdzisław Krasnodębski respectively, as well as by one frontline section of Cpt. Stefan Łaszkiewicz. Two Polish airmen, including Grzegorz Sołogub, a future ace, who rests against the wing, were photographed at Mions aerodrome with this type of aircraft.

Cpt. Kosiński's Section defending Bourges and flying Curtiss Hawk H.75. L-R: Cpl. Wacław Giermer, Plt. Com. Władysław Majchrzyk, Lt. Wacław Łapkowski, Lt. Marian Wesołowski, Cpt. Bronisław Kosiński, Cpl. Adolf Pietrasiak, Sub. Lt. Jan Daszewski, Cpl. Jan Kremski, Cpl. Zygmunt Rozworski. Out of this group only Giermer and Majchrzyk survived the war.

Morane Saulnier MS. 230 no. 823 flown by the Polish pilot who crash-landed at Montpellier on 17 May 1940.

MS.406 no. I, photographed on 17 June 1940 after Cpt. Tadeusz Opulski's unlucky take off, when the aircraft lost its right undercarriage leg. The landing could have ended much worse. The pilot commanded the Polish Section DAT defending Romorantin. Together with Sub. Lt. Jan Daszewski he claimed the first shared victory for the Poles of this unit.

Poles of the so-called 'Montpellier Group' or 'Montpellier Flight' photographed at Lyon-Bron aerodrome on 27 March 1940, after completing their training and right before being sent to the front line GCs. L–R: Lt. Józef Brzeziński, Sub. Lt. Erwin Kawnik, Cpt. Mieczysław Sulerzycki, Cpt. Stefan Łaszkiewicz, Cne. Jacques Rougevin-Baville (French instructor), Sgt. Leopold Flanek, Sub. Lt. Wacław Król, Sub. Lt. Stanisław Chałupa, Sub. Lt. Bolesław Rychlicki, Plt. Com. Antoni Beda, Sub. Lt. Bohdan Anders, Lt. Stefan Zantara. Note Morane MS.406 in the background, including aircraft no. 15.

Morane Saulnier MS. 406s with the Polish red and white chequers lined up at Lyon-Bron. MS. 406 no. 1031 (closest to camera) soon became the usual aircraft of Lt. Kazimierz Bursztyn. Flying this MS.406 he was shot down and wounded on 12 May 1940, and the aircraft was destroyed. The next one is no. 948 that was Sub. Lt. Władysław Chciuk's mount. Chciuk was downed on 16 May 1940 in this aircraft, but survived and returned to his unit. No. 948 had 'Always with God' stencilled in Polish on its fin.[1]

The same occasion, MS. 406s photographed at Lyon-Bron. The MS. 406 first from the left is no. 7 of the Depot d'Instruction de l'Aviation Polonaise and was used to train GC 1/145 pilots.

Sgt Leopold Flanek, one of the 'Montpellier Flight's' men, was posted to GCIII/2 where, on 10 May 1940 he claimed the destruction of a Bf 110. Six days later he was last seen when shooting down a Dornier, yet the victory was never confirmed. The pilot could not claim it as he was killed when his MS 406 crash-landed in Neuvillette in Ardennes.

Despite being known as the only Polish unit operationally flying Caudron CR. 714s, GC 1/145's pilots also used other types of aircraft. Cpl. Edward Uchto from Section No. 3/ Flight No. 2 photographed with MS 406C1 no. 901 '4', L-930 used for training at Lyon-Mions. Uchto was killed in action on 9 June 1940 while flying C.714, alongside two other pilots: Lt. Jan Obuchowski and Sub. Lt. Lech Lachowicki-Czechowicz. All were downed by II./JG 27. Another pilot of GC 1/145, Lt. Julian Kowalski, was wounded. The unit claimed four enemy aircraft destroyed and two probably on that day.

Caudron-Renault CR.714 'Cyclone' serial no. 8546 I-204, no. 14, white '2' of the DIAP Lyon, with the Polish chequer painted over the French roundel. The unlucky pilot was most probably Sub. Lt. Franciszek Kornicki, who recalled the circumstances of the crash-landing in this aircraft at St. Symphorien d'Ozon airfield a long time after the war.

MS.406 no. 1031 (L-621), code no. I of Lt. Kazimierz Bursztyn, who is sitting in flying gear, pictured in April 1940 at Rouen-Boss. The Polish pilot led the section attached to GCIII/1. Note the emblem of the 1st Escadrille GCIII/1 below the windscreen. Bursztyn was wounded in action while flying no. 1031 on 12 May 1940 and hospitalised. He returned to GCIII/1 thirteen days later and during an afternoon combat with Bf 109s he was killed in action.

Sub. Lt. Władysław Chciuk's MS. 406 no. 948 (L-979), code no. III with the emblem of a Winking Fox of the 1st Escadrille GCIII/1. Note the application of the Polish Air Force emblem which is not in accordance with the regulations implemented on 1 December 1918 and then on 1 March 1930. This was rather individually treated since the early days and will be seen in this book frequently.

Bloch MB. 152 serial no. 656 code no. 1 (note a red '1'with the white outline on the fin) flown by Lt. Zdzisław Henneberg, DAT Châteauroux. Later the white '1' number was applied on the fuselage; such marked aircraft was flown by Henneberg to Britain, when France capitulated. MB. 152 no. 656 was taken over by the RAF and repainted accordingly.

Koolhoven FK. 58 no. 11 of the so-called 'Jasionowski Flight', named after its commander, Cpt. Walerian Jasionowski. No. 11 was delivered in early June and flown (among others) by Lt. Bohdan Grzeszczak. This picture was taken by the Germans at the Montpellier aerodrome (note Junkers Ju 52 in the background).

Despite many Polish fighter pilots participating in operations, only two of their units received Dewoitine D. 520s. One of them was a group of Poles posted to GCII/7. This photo shows Maj. Mieczysław Mümler's personal aircraft no. 119 with the white 'M' letter, found by the German troops at Ounans. Mümler was one of the most experienced Polish fliers, and he was attached to GCII/7 for stage only, yet he managed to claim three victories (two of them when flying D.520) on 25 May, 1 June and finally on 15 June, when he was brought down. After an emergency landing, he was initially captured as a spy by the French gendarmerie.

Three Caudron CR. 714s out of the GC 1/145's fifteen aircraft[2] left at Dreux airfield and captured by the Germans. No. 13, serial no. 8544 'I-202' was flown by Sub. Lt. Bolesław Gładych, while No. 10 serial no. 8543 'I-201' was Cpl. Andrzej Niewiara's mount. The third fighter in the backdrop is No. 7 serial no. 8555, I-213 usually flown by Lt. Zdzisław Zadroziński. All of these pilots belonged to the Flight II, with Gładych and Niewiara being in Section No. 1 and Zadroziński commanding Section No. 3.

Chapter 3

Battle of Britain

Perhaps this Hurricane I N2359 has very little to do with the Polish pilots, as there is no evidence of any of the PAF officers posted to No. 17 Sqn RAF flying it. However the emblem of a winged Popeye had more Polish roots than many in this unit would have thought. Popeye, the cartoon character, had been very popular since 1929 when it was created in the USA, but it was based on Polish emigrant Franciszek Figiel (later Frank Fiegel aka 'Rocky'), a Chester-based barman, doorman and local troublemaker on one hand, a great friend of children on another. Somehow Poland born Popeye, a big fan of spinach, flew over England during the Battle of Britain.

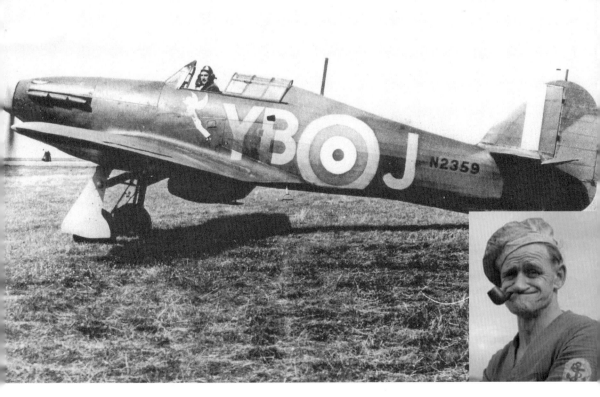

Pilots of No. 74 Sqn RAF photographed with their commander, Sqn Ldr Adolph 'Sailor' Malan, and Spitfire I K9953 ZP-A that, in August 1940, was flown by Flg Off Henryk Szczęsny. The latter, due his tongue-breaking surname was called 'Sneezy' or 'Henry the Pole'. Szczęsny, as well his colleague Flt Lt Stanisław 'Breezy' Brzezina, were pre-war fighter tactics instructors with countless hours of flying experience[1].

Spitfire Is of No. 65 Sqn. Flg Off Władysław Szulkowski flew R6712 YT-N frequently and used it to destroy a Bf 109 on 22 August 1940. The second aircraft s/n R6714 YT-M was flown by both Szulkowski and Flg Off Franciszek Gruszka, before the latter was shot down and killed on 18 August 1940 while in R6713. Szulkowski was joined by another Pole, Plt Off Bolesław Drobiński, and stayed with No. 65 Sqn for a few months after the Battle of Britain. On 26 November 1940 he was wounded in a landing accident in Spitfire R6987.

Hawker Hurricane I V7434 DZ-R of No. 151 Sqn was flown by Plt Off Gustaw Radwański on 14 September 1940, only two days after the Polish pilot was posted to this unit. In October he was transferred to No. 607 and soon to 56 Sqns RAF. In the latter squadron 'Gucio' Radwański served till May 1941, claiming one Do 17 damaged on 6 April.

Among the few Polish pilots posted to No. 32 Sqn RAF was Sgt Wilhelm Sasak, who flew Hurricane I P3981 GZ-W, pictured here. Later he was reposted to No. 145 Sqn RAF and was killed while flying back from operational sortie on 30 November 1940.

Hurricane I R4218 UF-U, a usual mount of Flg Off Juliusz Topolnicki of No. 601 Sqn. This aircraft was occasionally used by his colleague Flg Off Jerzy Jankiewicz, the only Polish Battle of Britain pilot who flew Hurricanes before. In July and August 1939 Jankiewicz visited Britain to test RAF aircraft ordered by Poland. Upon arrival in his homeland he was appointed Hawker Hurricane instructor, but unfortunately neither Hurricanes nor Spitfires ever arrived. Both: Topolnicki and Jankiewicz have not seen the end of war, Topolnicki lost his life on 21 September 1940 while in No. 601 Sqn; Jankiewicz on 25 May 1942 while commanding No. 222 Sqn RAF.

Two Hawker Hurricanes of No. 501 Sqn taking off. During the Battle of Britain, few Polish pilots served in this unit: Sgt Antoni Głowacki, Plt Off Franciszek Kozłowski, Sgts Mieczysław Marcinkowski and Konrad Muchowski, Plt Off Stanisław Skalski, Plt Off Paweł Zenker and Flg Off Stefan Witorzeńć. Both Głowacki and Kozłowski flew Hurricane P3208 SD-T, while P3059 SD-N was piloted by Głowacki and Zenker. The latter went missing during an operational sortie on 24 August 1940 while in Hurricane P3141 SD-W.

The majority of Polish names caused a headache to their British colleagues, who found it easier to use various nicknames: in the case of No. 609 Sqn, Flg Off Tadeusz Nowierski and Piotr Ostaszewski-Ostoja were called 'Novi' and 'Osti' or 'Post' respectively. The latter returned from a combat mission on 25 August 1940 wounded in badly damaged Spitfire R6986 PR-S.

Flg Off Witold Głowacki of No. 605 Sqn flew an operational sortie on 24 September 1940 when he spotted an enemy bomber. The Pole chased it from Beachy Head to Cap Gris Nez where the E/A crashed. The Pole was subsequently attacked by the Bf 109s and crash-landed near Albermouse. The series of photos depicting his Hurricane I P3832 UP-P were taken by the German troops. Głowacki was taken to hospital where he died the same day.

For the next few years Hurricanes and Spitfires coded WX-L became official mounts of No. 302 Squadron COs, where an individual letter 'L' stood for 'Leader'. This habit began during the Battle of Britain, when the British Commander, Sqn Ldr William Satchell, started to use this Hawker Hurricane I V6865 WX-L as his personal mount. The role of No. 302 Squadron is often underestimated, which results from a comparison with No. 303 Sqn operating within No. 11 Fighter Group, being crucial for the Battle. Had, however, the German attack come from Norway and Holland, the engagement of No. 12 Group and subsequently No. 302 Sqn would have been much more intense.

No. 303 Sqn is considered one of the most successful units of the Battle of Britain. Unfortunately their great achievements came with a price. 'City of Warsaw. Tadeusz Kościuszko' Squadron lost six of their own men in combat.[2] The very first losses occurred on 11 September 1940 when Flg Off Arsen Cebrzyński and Sgt Stefan Wójtowicz did not return from their operational sortie. The latter flew Hurricane I V7242 RF-B, pictured here. Before he crashed near Westerham, he destroyed a Bf 109 and probably destroyed another.

Hawker Hurricane I V6577 RF-P had a short operational career during the Battle of Britain. It was delivered to replace P3089 RF-P which crashed on 7 October 1940, when Plt Off Bogusław Mierzwa was returning from an operational sortie. Sgt Jan Kowalski took off in V6577 three days later to participate in patrol for the first time. The same pilot used this aircraft next day during operational mission and then, a few hours later, when the whole squadron flew to RAF Leconfield for rest. Here V6577, which remained with the unit until their conversion to Spitfires, is photographed on 15 December 1940 when AM William Sholto Douglas (pictured here whilst giving a speech) decorated four No. 303 Sqn pilots with the DFC. Sqn Ldr Adam Kowalczyk (Polish commander) stands second from left; Sqn Ldr Ronald G. Kellett is third.

Chapter 4

PAF Reborn. Under Skies of Britain and Europe
(Polish Air Force Squadrons Formed Between 1940–1941)

No. 302 'CITY OF POZNAŃ' SQUADRON

No. 302 was not only the first Polish fighter squadron, but also the second PAF unit formed under British command[1]. This squadron used a badge consisting of a raven, which was an emblem of fighter units from the 3rd Air Regiment in Poznań, where many of 302's first members originated, but also used colours of a French flag, and number '1/145' to commemorate the air battles fought across the Channel, where the core of the initial crew flew[2]. No. 302 Sqn was formed at RAF Leconfield and, as many believe due to its location (including operations from RAF Duxford), the unit missed a big part of the Battle of Britain. However at the time of allocation to No. 12 Group, the German tactics were a mystery, and attack from Norway and Holland equally possible. In this picture, taken in early 1941, a group of No. 302 Sqn pilots was photographed with a Hawker Hurricane I V7045 WX-V. L–R: Sgt Marian Rytka, Plt Off Marceli Neyder, Sgt Antoni Beda, Flg Off Władysław Gnyś and Flg Off Marian Duryasz. The latter three were Battle of Britain veterans[3], with Beda and Gnyś having combat experience from France. This aircraft had an individual code letter 'A' and in December 1941, Flt Lt John A. Finnis, Flight Commander from RAF, probably destroyed a Ju 88.

The same men posing in front of a V7045 WX-V. Note the black (Night) under surface of the port wing, the change that was, as well as Sky propeller spinner and Sky band on the rear fuselage, introduced in November 1940 on day fighters.

Hurricane I V6744 WX-C was delivered to No. 302 Sqn during the Battle of Britain but only on 4 March 1941 had its better moment, when Flg Off Julian 'Roch' Kowalski claimed damage of a Ju 88 when flying it. Note the application of the PAF chequer below the canopy, typical for this unit and period of time between 1940 and 1943, as well as the location of the squadron's code letters painted between RAF roundel and Sky band, that also changed in 1943. No. 302's emblem started to appear in early 1943, but at the beginning of 1944 this process had stopped. The raven on the blue, white and red diamond-shaped background appeared once more, but during the after the war service.

Mk II serial no. Z2342 WX-F was to replace P6742 and was first flown on 10 March 1941 by Sgt Antoni Łysek. Often used by Plt Off Władysław Kamiński, but also by Sgt Robert Nastorowicz and Plt Off Aleksander Narucki. On 28 March Kamiński participated in shared destruction of a Ju 88A-5 3Z+EN from II./KG 77 when flying this aircraft. On 29 April: 'Sgt pilot [Marian] Domagała was flying Hurricane Z.2342, at 27,000 ft over Dungeness, when his engine stopped and white smoke escaped from the exhaust pipes. Attempts to start the engine failed and he eventually landed at R.A.F. Biggin Hill. Owing to loss of speed he made a heavy landing and the aircraft was damaged. Cat.B. The pilot was uninjured.'[4]

Hurricane II Z2667 WX-E photographed at RAF Westhampnett in April 1941. This aircraft was flown by various pilots of No. 302 Sqn, before being sent to No. 43 Sqn RAF, where two Poles – Plt Off Franciszek Czajkowski and Sgt Zygmunt Rozworski – flew this mount too. Note the lack of a PAF badge!

When flying Hurricane II Z2668 WX-H, Plt Off Stanisław Łapka claimed a shared victory. On 28 March 1941, together with Plt Off Władysław Kamiński and Sgt Antoni Łysek, he downed a Ju 88A-5 3Z+EN from II./KG 77 in the area of St Catherine's Point.

Another Mk II Hurricane that arrived at No. 302 Sqn in March 1941. In this picture a major change can be seen: the whole under surface is in Sky colour, and the black paint, which was applied under the port wing between November 1940 and April 1941, has gone. Hurricane IIA Z3095 WX-N was photographed at RAF Kenley in April 1941. Flying this aeroplane Flg Off Zygmunt Kinel claimed destruction of a Messerschmitt Bf 109[5] in the area of Maidstone. Unfortunately the Polish pilot was killed on the same day during an afternoon encounter, sitting in the cockpit of Z3095.[6]

Hurricane II Z3675 WX-B was delivered to No. 302 Sqn in August 1941. On 4 September 1941 Plt Off Kazimierz Sporny probably downed a Bf 109 while flying it. During the same mission his commander, Sqn Ldr Stefan Witorzeńć, destroyed another German fighter of the same type. These were not only the last victories achieved by 'City of Poznań' Squadron when using Hurricanes, but by any other Polish fighter pilot flying aircraft of this type during the Second World War. Also No. 302 Squadron was the last day fighter unit of the PAF converting from Hurricanes to Spitfires, and the transformation was completed on 30 October 1941. Picture was taken after Z3675 delivery to Soviet Union.

Spitfire VB AD257 WX-A was a presentation aircraft 'Borough of Willesden' and on 30 December 1941 it was flown by Flg Off Czesław Główczyński, who scored a Bf 109. This was only one out of five claims made during Veracity II by 'City of Poznań' pilots (the first successes since conversion to a new type), and thirteen made by the Polish pilots in total during this operation.

Unlike their British comrades, the Polish airmen left their loved ones over 1,000 miles away. No surprise then that quite often they adorned their aircraft with the sweethearts' names. In this case Spitfire V AB872 WX-K 'Janeczka' (diminutive of a female name Janina). Fitter Cpl. Piotr Skrzypczak is sitting on a wing. With time, when their English language improved, the Poles were able to approach the local girls and their names started to appear on fuselages too.

Spitfire VB AA850 probably WX-U or WX-H that was flown by Plt Off Marian Rytka on 17 April 1942 when the pilot was credited with the destruction of a Bf 109.

Plt Off Eugeniusz Nowakiewicz fought three major air battles: over Poland, France and Battle of Britain, before being commissioned. He was shot down by ground fire and wounded while flying Spitfire VB BL549 WX-E over France on 23 July 1942. After force landing at Equihen-Plage Nowakiewicz was helped by the locals, but during his trip to Paris he was captured by the Gestapo.

Spitfire LF.VB BM648 was delivered brand new to No. 302 Sqn in June 1942 and coded WX-R. This aircraft was adorned with a (possible) female name of 'Baśka' or 'Kaśka' [diminutive of Polish Barbara or Katarzyna (Catherine)]. BM648 survived for almost a year to be transferred to No. 308 Sqn. During 'Jubilee' Operation this aircraft participated in three sorties, being flown by Flg Off Tadeusz Kwiatkowski, Plt Off Marian Rytka and Flg Off Eugeniusz Ebenrytter respectively.

RAF Heston, July 1942. Plt Off Mieczysław Gorzula is talking to a ground crew member. The aircraft that is partially obscured by 'Mike' is Spitfire VB AR385 WX-J, another Spitfire employed during Dieppe Raid. It was used twice by Sgt Eustachy Łucyszyn and twice by Plt Off Andrzej Beyer. This machine was lost on 24 April 1943 with Flt Lt Józef Dec inside cockpit, after Spitfire EN828 WX-E, piloted by Plt Off Czesław Nowak, hit AR385's tail with the propeller. Note Spitfire AR434 SZ-J from Polish No. 316 Squadron in the background (see No. 316 Squadron Chapter).

Spitfire VB W3902 WX-T arrived at No. 302 Sqn in October 1941 and it was used by this unit until June 1943. A photo session at RAF Heston in September 1942 shows a staged scramble, but W3902 WX-T was also used for a well-known propaganda poster…

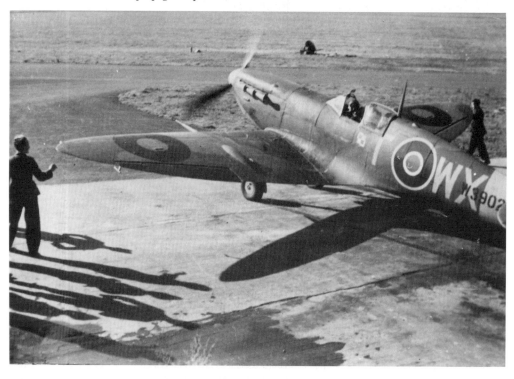

... of Plt Off Bogdan Muth leaving the cockpit of W3902 WX-T. Another staged photo that shows what is supposed to be a 'return from a sortie'. This shot was used for the 'Poland. First to Fight' placard. W3902 had also a small episode during Operation 'Jubilee' flying short patrol only.

Spitfire VB W3954 WX-B with the characteristic style of a serial number application. During the Dieppe Raid this aircraft was piloted by Sgt Kazimierz Benziński. On 7 September 1942 No. 306 'City of Toruń' Squadron's Sgt Jan Rogowski⁷had a landing accident at RAF Manston in it, breaking the undercarriage. W3954 was flown by another Polish pilot, Flg Off Bolesław Palej, ferrying this mount from No. 504 Sqn RAF to No. 14 OTU and who also had a landing accident in this aeroplane colliding with cows. The pilot was seriously injured; the condition of the cattle remains a mystery. In 1943, when still with No. 302 Sqn, the individual code letter was changed to 'O'.

RAF Croydon, early July 1942. One of No. 302 Squadron Spitfires, presumably AA850, is being prepared for Operation 'Rutter'. Four white vertical bands' awaiting their application on the forward fuselage. Wg Cdr Stefan Janus, leading No. 1 Wing and Sqn Ldr Witold Urbanowicz, attached to the Wing, can be seen in a background third and fourth from left respectively.

Spitfire VB AA853 WX-C already in full 'Rutter' markings, ordered by Fighter Command for 11 Group aircraft. Quite often erroneously misinterpreted as 'Jubilee' Raid quick recognition bands, but in fact the Dieppe landing and its air cover took place six weeks later. This aircraft flew two sorties during the latter operation, flown by Plt Offs Andrzej Beyer and Jerzy Urbański respectively (obviously without white bands!).

A puzzling photo of Spitfire VB AA854 WX-G that was captured in the summer of 1942. This aircraft has unusual light camouflage applied onto typical upper surface colours. Sgt Hipolit Mikusek, pictured here in the cockpit, was shot down in this aircraft over France on 8 September 1942 and captured. Before his luck ran out, he flew two sorties in this mount during the air cover of the Dieppe assault.

Another example of No. 302's Spitfire VB that was delivered to No. 302 Sqn in July 1942. AD317 WX-K took part in the Dieppe Raid, being flown three times over France: twice by Flg Sgt Kazimierz Kobusiński and once by Sgt Mikusek. Returning from a sweep over Abbeville – Le Treport on 11 October 1942, Flg Off Tadeusz Ciastuła, without injuries, crash-landed in this aircraft in Heston Park. Later AD317 was used by No. 303 Sqn.

A series of photos (out of quite a few that were taken) showing Spitfire VB EN865 WX-L delivered to 'City of Poznań' Squadron in June 1942, photographed while it was the personal mount of Sqn Ldr Stanisław Łapka (leading a group of pilots riding bikes). Since Sqn Ldr William Satchell the aircraft coded 'L' for Leader became No. 302 commanders' mount, having not much in common with the initials of Piotr Łaguna or Stanisław Łapka. Note the application of the squadron's badge. Łapka flew EN865 during Operation 'Jubilee' on 19 August 1942, but by then he commanded A Flight and EN865 was Sqn Ldr Julian Kowalski's aircraft.

A group of No. 302 Squadron pilots photographed with Spitfire VB BM179 WX-A adorned with the female name Patricia, stencilled on the port side of the fuselage, partially obscured by the third pilot's hat. Interestingly aircraft P8742 WX-A had similar looking 'art' applied in the same location. This Spitfire flew two sorties during Operation 'Jubilee', piloted by Plt Off Jerzy Urbański (second from left) and then by Sgt Ignacy Czajka. BM179 crash-landed on 7 September, 1942 at Manston after a sweep over Dunkirk and Ostend. Its pilot, Sgt Czajka, was injured and admitted to hospital.

No. 303 'CITY OF WARSAW. TADEUSZ KOŚCIUSZKO' SQUADRON

After achieving a huge success during the Battle of Britain, No. 303 Squadron was sent to 'rest' at RAF Leconfield (and to replace No. 302 Sqn sent to RAF Northolt). Flying patrols and extensive training were the main duties there. The ground crews had much less battle damage to repair.

In November 1940, 303's Hurricanes received a makeover, as the other day fighter squadrons, repainting spinners into Sky, added a tail band in the same colour, as well as black under the surface of the port wing. This process can be seen in this photo (where a crew member is wearing a French leather jacket)[8].

Flg Off Jerzy Jankiewicz flew Hurricanes in July and August 1939 during his posting to Britain to test these fighters. A year later he fought in the Battle of Britain, also flying Hurricanes of No. 601 Squadron. On 23 October 1940 he was posted to No. 303 Squadron. Here he is, photographed with Mk I N2460 RF-D, which was used by this squadron from October to the end of December 1940.

One of the most photographed Hurricanes of No. 303 Sqn, V6684 RF-F. This mount had participated in a photographic session at RAF Leconfield and was adorned with 'The Polish Squadron 126 kills' and Hitler's caricature chalked on its fuselage, next to the squadron's emblem. But there was also a small motif applied on the engine cowling, only partially visible in this picture. There is no surprise that this aircraft was chosen to be the background for the propaganda photos, as it was used to score two Do 17s, two Bf 109s, one He 111, one Ju 88 and one Bf 110 by four 303 Sqn pilots: A/Sqn Ldr Witold Urbanowicz, Plt Off Jan Zumbach, Flt Lt John Kent and Flg Off Zdzisław Henneberg.

Hawker Hurricane I W9129 RF-W, that arrived in No. 303 on 5 January 1941 (hence lack of squadron's badge in this photo). Seventeen days later it was flown by Flg Off Wacław Łapkowski[9] (accompanied by Plt Off Wiktor Strzembosz, Hurricane I R4081 RF-O) during Operation 'Mosquito' in the Abbeville – Crecy area. As well as damaging at least one Bf 109 on the ground, 'Foka', as Łapkowski was called, brought 25 yards of a high-tension electric cable from France, wrapped around the fuselage and wings (not to mention damaged radiator and propeller). A typical Polish cavalry charge! On the same day the first Spitfire Is arrived, starting conversion period.

Hurricanes V7619 RF-M and P3162 RF-T (the latter still without 'Kościuszko' badge) took part in last operational sortie on 2 February 1940 flown by No. 303 Sqn in full strength of twelve Hurricanes. The next mission was carried by an A Flight of Spitfires and a B Flight using Hurricanes. The latter ones disappeared from this unit for a few months, making No. 303 not only the first PAF, but also first non-British unit flying Spitfires.

Plt Off Jan Zumbach photographed with a Spitfire Mk I R6975 RF-A, one of the first aircraft of this type delivered to No. 303 Sqn on 22 January 1941. R6975 was previously 'owned' by No. 64 Squadron RAF. Zumbach is frequently named a 'Swiss pilot of 'Kościuszko' Squadron', while it was his grandfather who settled in Poland at the end of the nineteenth century, and Jan was born and raised in Ursynów, near Warsaw.[10]

Another example of a Spitfire I used by No. 303 Sqn. The photo was taken while the unit had A Flight flying Mk Is and B Flight already converted onto IIAs. On 14 March 1941, Col. Merian Cooper paid a visit to RAF Northolt and was welcomed by the already famous unit that originated from the 7th 'Kościuszko' Squadron[11] operating between 1919–1921 against the Bolsheviks. Cpt. Cooper[12] was one of the American volunteers of the latter, and his colleague Lt. Elliott Chess designed the 'Kościuszko' badge of two crossed scythes symbolising Tadeusz Kościuszko's Uprising against the Russians in 1794, with the red stripes and blue stars reflecting the latter fighting for American independence. Such an emblem, with small changes, was not only applied on 303's aircraft but it is still being used in the Polish Air Force to this day.[13] In this photo Cooper is photographed with Plt Offs Mirosław Ferić and Jan Zumbach. The latter scored the first Spitfire victory for No. 303 while in N3059 RF-F, used here as a background. Unfortunately his claim was never accepted. Note the application of the unit's badge behind the canopy, typical for early Mk Is in this unit.

Sqn Ldr Zdzisław Henneberg in the cockpit of Spitfire IIA P7746 RF-B 'CITY OF BRADFORD I'

Spitfire IIA P8029 RF-P, used for the background for this photo, was lost in the Channel on 12 April 1941 with Sqn Ldr Zdzisław Henneberg. L-R: Plt Off Bolesław Drobiński, Flg Off Wiktor Strzembosz (who flew with Flt Lt Wacław Łapkowski searching for his commander and, while doing so, both were attacked by 10 Bf 109s)[14], Sgt Matěj Pavlovič,[15] Flg Off Jarosław Giejsztowt (Intelligence Officer) and Sgt Marian Bełc. Out of four pilots posing here, only Drobiński survived the war.

Flg Off Wojciech Kołaczkowski, B Flight commander, captured with his Spitfire IIA P8038 RF-W for Wojtek. When in the middle of May 1941, Spitfire IIBs, armed with four machine guns and two Hispano guns, started to arrive, IIAs were allocated to No. 452 Squadron RAAF. Note that the Squadron's emblem went under the cockpit.

P8038 became the personal aircraft of Flt Lt Brendan 'Paddy' Finucane. Note that the aircraft is still adorned with the 'Kościuszko' badge. The code letters 'RF' were changed to 'UD', however the individual letter 'W' remained. It is believed that the Polish motif was replaced by 'Paddy's' symbol – a green shamrock.

An interesting photo of a IIA P8085 RF-J while taxiing at RAF Northolt, which shows that an attempt has been made to apply the squadron's badge behind the canopy – typically for early days of flying Spitfires (hence empty disc) – but eventually the 'Kosciuszko' scythes and American stars are in correct position. P8085 was one of many presentation aircraft used by No. 303, note: 'GARFIELD WESTON VII'.

Another presentation aircraft P8041 RF-E, named 'NORTHAMPTON' was Plt Off Jan Daszewski's lucky Spitfire when, on 20 April 1941, he was credited with the destruction of a Bf 109.

Spitfire II P7962 RF-A 'INSPIRATION' was shot down on 9 May 1941 and its pilot, Plt Off Jan Zumbach, baled out. A few hours earlier, P7962, flown by Plt Off Bolesław Gładych, was attacked by Hurricanes! Here, Sgt Mieczysław Popek is standing in the cockpit.

Spitfire IIB P8507 RF-V became Sqn Ldr Wacław Łapkowski's personal mount. Later this presentation aircraft, 'BERMUDA I', was re-coded to RF-Q, before being transferred to No. 306 'City of Toruń' Squadron. When there, on 29 August 1941, Sqn Ldr Jerzy Słoński-Ostoja was killed in action in this aeroplane. While in No. 303 Łapkowski scored four Bf 109s flying this mount and Sgt Stanisław Bełza claimed one Bf 109 probably destroyed. Standing L-R are: Plt Offs Bolesław Drobiński, Stefan Paderewski and Bolesław Gładych; sitting are: Flg Off Wojciech Kołaczkowski, Flt Lt Jerzy Jankiewicz and Flg Off Wilhelm Wittels from RAF.

Assigned to Wg Cdr John Kent, who was Wing Commander Flying of the Northolt Wing, Spitfire IIB P8189 was coded accordingly: RF-J (for John). On 22 June 1941, Sgt Józef Szlagowski collided with P8334 RF-E, piloted by Plt Off Maciej Lipiński while in the air. Both landed safely. Just the day before, Kent reported destruction of a Bf 109 in this aircraft.

Photo taken at RAF Northolt either on 24 June 1941, after arrival of No. 308 'City of Cracow' Squadron from RAF Chilbolton to join No. 1 Polish Wing, or a day later, but certainly before 3pm. Plt Off Stefan Paderewski, wearing a scarf, seen here right under the Spitfire IIB P8346 RF-T's tail, was killed in action on that day. Aircraft visible in the middle is believed to be P8331 RF-M 'SUMATRA', flying which Wg Cdr Piotr Łaguna (Polish commander of No. 1 Wing, here in a forage cap, almost directly below P8331) was killed on 27 June 1941. Spitfire on far right is P8333 RF-S 'BANDA'. P8346 'OSSETT AND HORBURY' was also lost to German flak within days, killing Plt Off Józef Bondar on 28 June.

Pictured here is the usual mount of Flg Off Mirosław Ferić, who gained a victory in it over a Bf 109. There were also other men of 'Kościuszko' Squadron helping this aircraft to be the lucky one: Sgt Józef Szlagowski (1 Bf 109 destroyed), Flt Lt Tadeusz Arentowicz (1 Bf 109 damaged) and Flg Off Jan Zumbach (1 Bf 109 destroyed and 1 Bf 109 probably destroyed). In this photo Plt Off Bronisław Kłosin poses with Spitfire IIB P8385 RF-A named 'IMPREGNABLE'. Note the application of a 'Pluto Dog' looking at a burning German aircraft – a personal emblem based on a Disney cartoon – but also the lack of the Polish chequer, which did not appear on 303's aircraft until early 1942.[16]

A less glamorous photo of a Polish-flown Spitfire IIB was taken in Belgium. This is either P8502 RF-C, flown for the last time by Sqn Ldr Tadeusz Arentowicz, when he went down near Dunkirk (initially thought to be lost in the sea), or P8669 RF-M, flown by Flg Off Wiktor Strzembosz, who was killed in the area of La Motte. Both pilots were lost on 9 July 1941 during another sortie of the so-called 'Non-Stop Offensive'.

Another interesting photo that shows not only the camouflage change to Grey and Green (note an individual code letter as well as female name 'Krysia' outlined with Dark Earth paint), but also the presence of a Hawker Hurricane Mk I in the background. While at RAF Speke both types were used again: Spitfire Is by Flight A and Hurricanes by Flight B. Spitfire I X4828 RF-K was Flt Lt Wojciech Kołaczkowski's (second right, wearing civilian clothes) mount adorned with his girlfriend's name 'Krysia' [diminutive of Polish Krystyna (English Christine)] as well as with his own name 'Wojtek' applied on the nose, below the exhaust pipes.

While at RAF Speke, No. 303 Sqn inherited Hurricane Is, previously flown by No. 315 'City of Dęblin' Squadron. These, alongside Spitfire Is (which started to arrive on 24 July 1941), were used for patrols and training. Sgt Mieczysław Popek crash-landed in P3932 RF-C dangerously close to the railway, owing his bad luck to an oil system failure.

October 1941 saw No. 303 Squadron's conversion to Spitfire Vs (No. 303 was the fourth PAF squadron to receive Mk. Vs) and a move back to RAF Northolt for the third time – no surprise then that many of the Poles called this place home. One of the unit's new fighters, VB W3764 RF-Q, with the name 'The Fun of the Fair', was usually flown by Plt Off Bolesław Gładych who, thanks to his accordion skills, was called 'Bemol'.

No. 303 Sqn pilots photographed with their Commander, Sqn Ldr Jerzy Jankiewicz, who is standing in the middle, holding Flt Lts Walerian Żak and Wojciech Kołaczkowski. This picture was taken upon return to Northolt in October 1941. Jankiewicz's personal Spitfire VB AD138 RF-T had been used as a background.

Picture of the same AD138 RF-T taken after Jankiewicz left No. 303 Sqn on 22 November 1941 and Sqn Ldr Kołaczkowski took his place. Plt Offs Adam Damm and Zbigniew Wojda are posing with it. Wojda was shot down over the Channel on 12 April 1942 and spent 30 minutes in a dinghy; his colleague was killed during Operation 'Jubilee'. Note the emblem of Pluto the Dog next to the squadron's badge. Spitfire AB929 RF-R can be seen in the background. This aircraft was flown on 24 October 1941 by Plt Off Bolesław Drobiński when he claimed one Bf 109 probably destroyed. The same pilot destroyed another Bf 109 on 13 March 1942 flying this mount.

Another aircraft adorned with Sqn Ldr Wojciech Kołaczkowski's name was W3765 RF-K. Here 'Wojtek' poses with Flt Lt Witold Łokuciewski nicknamed 'Tolo', A Flight commander (left) and Flt Lt Jan Daszewski, B Flight commander (right).

Spitfire VB AD116 RF-H with the presentation name 'TWICKENHAM I' was hit by a bullet which went directly through the cockpit on 15 November 1941. Luckily Flg Off Zygmunt Bieńkowski returned safe. Three No. 303 pilots scored in this aircraft: Flg Off Maciej Lipiński's the probable destruction of a Bf 109 on 13 March 1942; Flg Sgt Mieczysław Popek reported destruction of a FW 190 on 4 April 1942 and Plt Off Stanisław Socha probably destroyed Bf 109 eight days later. LAC Antoni Gulski is in the cockpit. Note the very basic version of the squadron's badge lacking stars.

Daszewski, called 'Long Joe', poses with Spitfire VB AB936 RF-V which he flew on 13 December 1941 when the aircraft was damaged by German flak and its pilot was wounded.

No. 303 Squadron personnel were left shaken on 14 February 1942 after the tragic loss of one of its most experienced members. Flying Officer Mirosław Ferić, also known as 'Ox', was a pilot of 111th Fighter Squadron in Poland (from which No. 303 Sqn originated), fighting against the Luftwaffe in 1939. He also started his personal diary by then which, in time, evolved as No. 303's official Chronicle. The circumstances of his death are still being analysed and discussed, even at the time of writing this book. He was killed after crashing in the middle of RAF Northolt tarmac runaway in Kołaczkowski's another personal Spitfire VB BL432 RF-K for 'Krysia'.

Although two FW 190s were downed by 'Kościuszko' pilots on 4 April 1942, the price was high. Flt Lt Jan Daszewski was killed, while Flt Lt Zbigniew Kustrzyński from 303's Ops Room was shot down and crash-landed in Spitfire VB AB824 RF-S in France, becoming a PoW.

Sgt Włodzimierz Chojnacki in the cockpit of Spitfire VB W3506 RF-U 'HENDON LAMB', which was lost when Plt Off Zbigniew Wojda was shot down on 12 April 1942. Despite being wounded, Wojda ditched his aircraft in the Channel to be rescued after half an hour.

Three Mk V Spitfires from No. 303 Squadron photographed at RAF Lindholme on 25 April 1942. At that time this aerodrome was a base for two Polish bomber squadrons, Nos. 304 and 305 (note a Wellington bomber in the distance). The three visiting 'Kościuszko' pilots were: Flt Lt Jan Zumbach in his personal BM144 RF-D, Sqn Ldr Wojciech Kołaczkowski in his BL670 RF-K 'Krysia' and Sgt Ryszard Górecki in BL375 RF-J 'Joan'.

Picture taken on the same occasion. Note the application of PAF markings. BL670 was a presentation Spitfire 'EVER READY II'. During the Dieppe assault aerial cover in August 1942, this aircraft (without 'Krysia' name, as Kołaczkowski handed command to Sqn Ldr Walerian Żak on 9 May 1942[17]) was flown twice: Plt Off Stanisław Socha scored one Ju 88 and one FW 190 in it, then Flg Sgt Mieczysław Popek shared the destruction of another FW 190.

Flt Lt Stefan Kołodyński was 38 when he was shot down and captured. Having a fighter pilot's career in 1930s, he was appointed flying instructor and then he graduated from the PAF Staff College. Despite this he decided to fly as an ordinary pilot of No. 303 Sqn and was brought down in Spitfire VB AA940 RF-E on 27 April 1942. Note an unusual application of sqn code letters.

On 9 May 9, 1942 Sqn Ldr Walerian Żak called 'Ciotka' (Aunt) took command of No. 303, however, his post did not last long, as three weeks later he was ordered to lead No. 308 Squadron. This picture of a Spitfire VB BM531 RF-V was taken at the same period of time.

Zumbach era! This charismatic pilot and recent A Flight commander was appointed to a new role on 17 May 1942. Almost a month later the whole squadron left for Kirton-in-Lindsey, but before this move a Spitfire VB AR335 RF-M was damaged while landing at Northolt with Sgt Alojzy Rutecki inside.

Sgt Arkadiusz Bondarczuk leaving the cockpit of Spitfire VB AA913 RF-P. In August 1942 this pilot was posted to No. 306 Squadron where, over a year later,[18] he was lost in the sea after being shot down by an enemy fighter. During Operation 'Jubilee', AA913 flew two missions piloted by Flg Sgt Jan Palak and Plt Off Zbigniew Wojda.

The squadron's dog, Misia, is looking after a war trophy: a fin panel standing on a port wing of Zumbach's VB BM144 RF-D. On 3 July 1942 two Ju 88s from 2./KüFlGr 106 were shot down by two sections of No. 303 Sqn (Flg Sgts Kazimierz Wünsche and Mieczysław Popek, Flg Off Tadeusz Kołecki and Sgt Aleksander Rokitnicki) and various parts (machine gun, dinghy paddle, life vest and Iron Cross) were collected. Interestingly the whole event description painted on German tail unit caught the attention of the censor and 'Kirton-in-Lindsey', as squadron location, was obliterated for the photos to be published.

Censorship work can be seen here. Popek and Rokitnicki, two recent victors, are posing with the tail unit, life vest and the Iron Cross.

Impressive scoreboard of Flg Sgt Mieczysław Adamek's kills can be seen here, despite the scenery, which depicts the troublesome day of 27 July 1942 for Plt Off Zbigniew Wojda in Spitfire VB AD198 RF-W. AD198 was previously flown as RF-J by Wg Cdr Stefan Janus of Northolt Wing.

Another unlucky pilot on the same day was Plt Off Stanisław Socha who crash-landed in Spitfire VB W3908 RF-C.

No. 303 Sqn pilots are being briefed by Sqn Ldr Jan Zumbach minutes before a Combined operation – 'Jubilee'. The unit's Spitfires can be seen in the background, including VB BL574 RF-F, soon to be flown by Sgt Józef Stasik to claim the destruction of a FW 190. In the afternoon, this aircraft would be lost and Plt Off Adam Damm killed.

Opposite: Two shots of No. 303 Sqn while operating within No. 2 Polish Wing, depicting Sqn Ldr Jan Zumbach in his Spitfire VB BM144 RF-D leading formation of: BM540 RF-I [letter 'I' expanded to female name, possibly Irena or its diminutive Irka (in English, Irene), hence in this photo looks like 'L'], AB183 RF-A, BL594 RF-G, BL567 RF-T and AR371 RF-B. Soon after this picture was taken BM144 was handed over to Flt Lt Zygmunt Bieńkowski and re-coded to RF-H for 'Halszka' as the individual code letter was extended. Halszka was a diminutive of Halina Grzybowska, Bieńkowski's fiancée. During aerial fights over Dieppe on 19 August 1942 Zumbach in his new RF-D, serial no. EP594, destroyed two FW 190s, one of them probably. In his final sortie he added a shared victory over a He 111. On that day Flt Lt Bieńkowski already operated in his BM144 RF-H, Plt Off Tadeusz Kołecki in AB183 RF-A destroyed one Ju 88, Flg Sgt Wacław Giermer in BM540 RF-I reported the probable destruction of a FW 190, then later a shared destruction of a He 111. Sgt Józef Karczmarz in BL567 RF-T also probably destroyed a FW 190. AR371 RF-B (adorned with the Polish female name Bronka applied on the nose) was flown by Flg Sgt Kazimierz Wünsche, then by Flg Sgt Mieczysław Popek, both without claims. BL594 RF-G was piloted by Flg Off Eugeniusz Horbaczewski, who reported one FW 190 shot down. No. 303 Sqn performed four missions during 'Jubilee', when RF-I and RF-A were also piloted by Sgts Ryszard Górecki and Józef Stasik respectively.

Even though being known as disastrous, Operation 'Jubilee', carried out on 19 August 1942, was one of the PAF's brightest moments. No. 303 Squadron downed nearly nine[19] enemy aircraft and four probably, gaining first place among the 45 squadrons involved.[20] All this with the loss of one of their own: Plt Off Adam Damm killed. Plt Off Stanisław Socha is looking at the damage to Spitfire VB AR366 RF-C, flown earlier on that day by his colleague, Sgt Aleksander Rokitnicki, who scored the shared destruction of a He 111, but brought back his aeroplane damaged. Previously the same AR366 was flown by Sgt Arkadiusz Bondarczuk. Socha had his glory as well, during 'Jubilee' he scored one FW 190 and one Ju 88 destroyed!

Picture taken at RAF Northolt shows another aircraft employed in Operation 'Jubilee'. Spitfire VB BM531 RF-V flying from Redhill operated over the target three times, piloted by Plt Off Mirosław Szelestowski, Sgt Alojzy Rutecki and once more by Szelestowski. Rutecki participated in the shared destruction of a He 111. Note Spitfire BL670 RF-K in the background, in which Plt Off Socha scored two kills on 19 August 1942. To the right BM540 RF-I or AR318 RF-L can be seen. The latter (by then coded RF-H) was a lucky aircraft of Sgt Józef Stasik when the pilot shot down a FW 190 on 5 June 1942, but also of Plt Off Tadeusz Kołecki, who scored the shared destruction of a Ju 88 on 7 July 1942. AR318 also flew two sorties during the Dieppe Raid, on both occasions piloted by Plt Off Czesław Mroczyk.

The same BM531 RF-V with Flg Off Bolesław Gładych personal score. Gładych was the usual pilot of this mount. Sgt Tadeusz Szymkowiak is in the cockpit.

Plt Off Antoni Głowacki gained his fame during the Battle of Britain when he scored five E/A in one day.[21] During aerial coverage of a Dieppe landing, he flew his personal mount Spitfire VC AB174 RF-Q ('QQWCA'[22]) twice, scoring one He 111 shared and a FW 190 probably destroyed.

BL748 RF-W, the third Spitfire usually flown by Flg Sgt Mieczysław Adamek, and was adorned with an individual code letter 'W'. When this picture was taken the pilot's score was: two shared kills from the Polish Campaign and five confirmed victories while in exiled PAF. During 'Jubilee' Adamek flew BL748 twice, but without results. Sgt Włodzimierz Chojnacki, who completed two sorties in RF-W on that day, also returned empty handed. Adamek was killed on 18 May 1944 when in No. 317 Sqn.

The very next day No. 303 flew back to Kirton-in-Lindsey where, on 1 September 1942, the squadron celebrated its second anniversary and was visited by Polish President in Exile, Władysław Raczkiewicz. Here, he is photographed during the mass sitting between two Spitfires: Sqn Ldr Jan Zumbach's new EP594 RF-D, with the scoreboard that includes pilot's kills from Dieppe Raid: 1 FW 190 destroyed, 1 FW 190 probably destroyed and 1 He 111 shared; on President's left is AB183 RF-A.

No. 306 'CITY OF TORUŃ' SQUADRON

Three Hawker Hurricane Mk Is of No. 306 Sqn, including V7118 UZ-V, photographed between 4 and 5 March 1941 at RAF Ternhill.

The same V7118 maintained by the ground crew. Note the application of the PAF chequer inside of the 'U' code letter, and squadron's badge on the engine cowling. No. 306 was the second Polish squadron that adorned their aircraft with the emblem. The latter consisted of a flying duck, reminiscencent of the unit's roots in 4th Air Regiment in Toruń, and a bear that symbolised No. 605 Sqn RAF from which Sqn Ldr Douglas Scott (306's British Commander) came from.

The same V7118, completely different application of the Polish national colours on port fuselage, between U and Z. Hurricanes V7743 UZ-D and R4104 UZ-F are in the background.

Better view of No. 306's emblem. This Hurricane has a glare shield for night flying, a very useful feature during late patrols. One of these missions proved succesful for Flg Off Władysław Nowak (first from left) who claimed the first victory for his squadron, during the night of 10/11 May 1941, shooting a He 111. Next to Nowak standing are: Sgts Jan Śmigielski and Otto Pudrycki; sitting is Sgt Leon Kosmowski.

Sqn Ldr Tadeusz Rolski's Hawker Hurricane R4101 UZ-F with the wide Sky band on the rear fuselage. Note that the black paint used to cover port underwing surface is fading off.

Hurricane V6986 UZ-U painted in colours introduced in November 1940 for a day fighter squadrons, meanwhile the aircraft in the background has still dark, most certainly black, spinner!

Sgt Jan Śmigielski is climbing into the cockpit of V7751 UZ-M with an unusually painted propeller hub. Note that the whole port under surface, including fuselage, is painted black. On 12 April 1941 the black colour was removed; it was when No. 306 Sqn already operated from RAF Northolt, being attached to No. 1 Polish Wing and re-equipped with Hurricane IIs (on 2 and 8 April[23] respectively).

Hawker Hurricane IIA Z3559 UZ-P. The squadron's emblem is in its usual location; however the PAF chequer is missing. This aircraft, as with the rest of the Hurricane IIs, was later handed over to No. 317 Sqn and coded JH-H.

On 11 and 12 July 1941, No. 306, led by Sqn Ldr Jerzy Zaremba, flew its last Hurricane sorties, and soon conversion to Spitfire IIs was completed. Picture shows landing mishap of Sgt Tadeusz Zawistowski, who, in a short period of time (between 28 August and 3 September 1941) twice crash-landed at Northolt. Note the lack of PAF chequer, previously applied between squadron code letters. Spitfire IIA P8025 UZ-R is adorned with squadron emblem. Zawistowski lost his life in an air collision on 11 September 1941.

Spitfire IIB P8462 UZ-M was piloted by Sgt Stanisław Zięba on 14 August 1941, when it was shot down over France and crashed at Belle-Houllefort. The Polish pilot was found alive and taken to Kriegsmarine hospital in Hardinghen, where he died of wounds nine days later. Note PAF red and white chequer applied between code letters.

After destroying a Bf 109 on 29 August 1941, Sgt Marcin Machowiak's Spitfire IIB P8342 UZ-N was severely damaged and the pilot had to land at Biggin Hill. P8342 was a presentation aircraft 'CERAM' with the personal emblem, probably linked to No. 145 Sqn RAF where it was previously flown. Another 306 pilot, Sgt Henryk Pietrzak, scored two Bf 109s in it (one destroyed, another damaged) two weeks before Machowiak's experience.

Sqn Ldr Jerzy Zaremba, who led No. 306 Sqn from 1 July 1941, was shot down and killed during the same sortie when Sgt Zięba was downed over France.[24] Sqn Ldr Jerzy Słoński-Ostoja – Zaremba's successor – who was victorious on 14 August 1941, survived him for only fifteen days. Similarly to Zaremba, Słoński also flew Spitfire IIB UZ-Z during his last sortie, but his aircraft was P8466's replacement and had serial number P8507. This tragic photo shows what was left of it.

RAF Northolt, 4 September 1941. A brand new Mk VB Spitfire delivered to No. 306 Sqn, while under command of Sqn Ldr Antoni Wczelik. Sgt Henryk Pietrzak and Plt Off Bronisław Wydrowski (a Battle of Britain veteran) are posing proudly with it. Note that the squadron's recognition markings are not yet applied.

Pilots of No. 306 Sqn seem to enjoy watching a new Mk V in the air, especially on Squadron's Day. From left to right are: Sgts Pietrzak, Jan Śmigielski, Stanisław Wieprzkowicz, Flt Lt Stanisław Zieliński (A Flight Commander), Sgt Otto Pudrycki, Flg Off Stanisław Marcisz, Sgts Józef Jeka, Leon Kosmowski and Marcin Machowiak. Only four of these men: Pietrzak, Śmigielski, Marcisz and Jeka would survive the war.

A year later, since receiving Spitfire Vs during the early days of September 1941, while in No. 1 Polish Wing at Northolt, the new appearance of their aircraft was evident with the PAF chequer on the engine cowling and the squadron's badge below the windscreen. With time the code letters were painted in opposite order: squadron code aft the windscreen and individual letter between RAF roundel and tail. But the majority of Mk Vs remained as in the picture of AA930 UZ-P with two Sgts: Wawrzyniec Jasiński and Marian Kordasiewicz. AA930 was flown on two sorties during Operation 'Jubilee' on 19 August 1942 by Plt Off Jerzy Polak and then by Flg Off Jan Kurowski.

Spitfire VB AA919 UZ-J was usually flown by Flg Off Bohdan Arct, but was lost on 14 April 1942 with its pilot Flg Off Edward Jankowski. During the same operation the Squadron's Commander Sqn Ldr Antoni Wczelik was also killed.

Spitfire VB AA858 UZ-D was flown by Sgt Leon Kosmowski during Operation 'Veracity' on 18 December 1941, when the Polish pilot claimed the destruction of a Bf 109. Seriously damaged on 1 May 1942, by German bombing of an airfield occupied by the Poles, AA858 was sent for repairs. Later this aircraft was used by No. 302 Squadron, but only for a short period of time.

Sgt Witold Krupa joined No. 306 Sqn in late 1941. Here he is posing with Spitfire VB AD304 UZ-G, which previously was used as the personal mount of Sqn Ldr Aleksander Gabszewicz, Commander of No. 316 Sqn and coded SZ-G. Gabszewicz flew it prior to receiving his consecutive Mk Vs: P8606 and then BL901 (both SZ-Gs). AD304 UZ-G was seen for the last time on 24 April 1942 when flown by Plt Off Adam Fliśnik, who failed to return from 'Rodeo 2'.

Flg Off Roman Pentz's Spitfire VB BL733 UZ-D was brought down by German flak during Ramrod near Boulogne in France on 30 July 1942. The pilot was captured.

At the end of June 1942, No. 306 Squadron was moved to RAF Croydon expecting to be engaged in Operation 'Rutter', the trial Allied landing in France to answer Joseph Stalin's demands to open the second front in Europe. Due to bad weather the operation was postponed. Both photos show No. 306 Sqn's Spitfire Vs, including VB AR336 UZ-O, adorned with 'Rutter' markings. This aircraft flew three sorties during 'Jubilee' Operation instead, piloted by Flg Off Witold Szyszkowski and twice by Sgt Marian Kordasiewicz.

The actual landing took place on 19 August 1942 and No. 306 Squadron flew four separate sorties over Dieppe. For 'City of Toruń' Squadron Operation 'Jubilee' proved to be less successful than for their colleagues from Nos. 303 and 317. Furthermore, Flg Off Emil Landsman (Spitfire BM424 UZ-S) was shot down and captured and Sgt Stefan Czachla, flying on fumes only, crashed in Ruislip, unable to reach RAF Northolt. Here, the wreckage of his Spitfire VB AD581 UZ-M is being watched by the residents of Malvern Avenue. The wounded pilot had already been taken away. Also Flg Off Arct's AR337 UZ-A has been damaged by flak.

No. 307 'CITY OF LWÓW. LWÓW EAGLE OWLS SQUADRON (NIGHT FIGHTER)

No. 307 'City of Lwów' Night Fighter Squadron, formed at RAF Kirton-in-Lindsey between 24 August and 5 September 1940, was initially supposed to be equipped with Hawker Hurricanes. Much to the pilots' disappointment, as many of them had combat experience on single seaters, it was decided that they would be 'drivers' only, and the only armament would be four 0.303 in Browning machine guns for the rear air gunner! Boulton Paul Defiant Mk I caused lot of havoc among the Polish personnel; many pilots, including the first Polish commander Sqn Ldr Stanisław Pietraszkiewicz, asked to be transferred elsewhere.

The initial role assigned to No. 307 Sqn was to fly convoy patrols, hence aircraft EW-K is wearing day fighter colours here.

Both photos of Defiant I N3437 EW-K show the aircraft at RAF Exeter, photographed in spring 1941. The crew Sgts Franciszek Jankowiak (pilot) and Józef Lipiński (gunner) posing next to the aeroplane converted into a night fighter role. Jankowiak, flying with Sgt Jerzy Karais on the night of 12/13 March 1941 claimed the first success for their unit by damaging a He 111. Crew photographed here gained the first 307's victory on 12 April 1941 by destroying a He 111 from 9./KG 27.

Defiant I N1684 EW-A was delivered to No. 307 Sqn in September 1940, but it was damaged beyond repair on 11 January 1941 at RAF Jurby by Sgt Ludwik Mirończuk, who was taxiing in N1699. Before the accident, the aircraft was last flown on short patrol on 1 January 1941 by the crew of Flt Lt Mieczysław Jakszewicz and Sgt Stanisław Jarzembowski. Why N1684 remained grounded for 10 days is a mystery.

Finally, in the summer of 1941, it was decided to get rid of Defiants and re-equip No. 307 Sqn with Bristol Beaufighters. Bristol Blenheim Mk I was chosen for the transition period and a few of them were delivered between 12 August and October 1941. Photo shows L8438 damaged on landing on 20 August 1941 by the crew of Plt Off Marceli Neyder and Flg Sgt Bolesław Turzański.

Opposite: Finally by the end of July 1941 the real fighters had arrived. Bristol Beaufighter IIFs designed for night fighting duties were enthusiastically received and it was finally the pilot deciding when and where to use four 20 mm Hispano cannons and six 0.303 in Browning machine guns! Here Sgt Bolesław Turzański is posing in front of IIF. Turzański and Sgt Henryk Ostrowski claimed two Do 217s on the night of 1/2 November 1941, opening the list of victories on a new type. A couple of nights before, the same crew probably destroyed an unrecognised aircraft. On 28 November they added one more unknown E/A. In all three cases they flew Beaufighter IIF R2379, probably pictured here. Turzański and Ostrowski scored one more victory, this time it was another Do 217 downed on 28 June 1942 while flying a Beaufighter VI.

Flg Off Jerzy Damsz photographed at RAF Exeter in May 1942. The aircraft behind are T3009 EW-B and T3382 EW-K, both IIFs. Flying T3382 Flg Offs Mieczysław Pietrzyk and Czesław Krawiecki reported probable destruction of a Ju 88 on 26 April 1942. T3009 was flown on 4 May 1942 by Flg Off Stanisław Andrzejewski and Sgt Stanisław Kaliszewski, when a Ju 88 was spotted and probably destroyed. The latter aircraft was damaged on landing on 7 January 1942 by Sgt Jerzy Malinowski. With time, Jerzy Damsz was appointed the last commander of No. 307 Squadron.

Beaufighter IIF T3048 EW-O was used by 'City of Lwów' Squadron between 15 December 1941 and 7 May 1942 when it was delivered to No. 96 Sqn RAF.

R2445 EW-A being repaired by the ground crews at RAF Exeter, following a tragic accident on 14 February 1942 when Plt Off Stefan Maxymowicz-Raczyński was killed and Flg Off Jerzy Łazarowicz seriously wounded. The latter was taken to hospital where a leg was amputated, and until his demobilisation he served as ground controller.

A formation of Beaufighter IIs photographed on 2 April 1942 with T3030 EW-N with the crew of Sqn Ldr Maksymilian Lewandowski and Sgt Tadeusz Śliwak, leading the rest. R2390 UZ-U piloted on that day by Flg Sgt Bolesław Turzański, accompanied by Sgt Henryk Ostrowski, is closer to the camera.

The same Beaufighter R2390 EW-U. Note the lack of a red and white chequer.

A distinctive difference, two radial Hercules engines and Airborne Interception Mk VIII radar, of a new type delivered to No. 307 Squadron. Mk VIFs were in use since May 1942. The aircraft in this photo is EL154 EW-Z.

No. 308 'CITY OF CRACOW' SQUADRON

Like most of the Polish day fighter squadrons,[25] No. 308 'City of Cracow' Squadron also started its history with this type of aircraft. Photos of No. 308 Hurricanes, however, are rare; those known do not provide much data to recognise particular aircraft especially because their serial numbers are not visible. During a photo session at RAF Badington, pilots 'efficiently' – purposely or ignorantly – obscured their fighter planes, making them hard to identify. In this photo Plt Off Tadeusz Hojden and Flg Off Władysław Chciuk are posing next to Hawker Hurricane I. Code letters are yet to be applied and only the first character of the serial number can be seen. Hojden was killed on 27 March 1941, while in No. 315 Sqn, Chciuk was shot down over France on 24 July 1941 and captured.

Thanks to squadron code 'ZF', No. 308 pilots were known as 'Zefyrs' among their PAF colleagues. The first core of RAF Squires Gate formed unit[26] came from the bunch of battle-hardened pilots with combat experience from Poland and then from France, including the first commander Sqn Ldr Stefan Łaszkiewicz (pictured in the middle; GCIII/2) and much taller Plt Off Bronisław Skibiński (112th Fighter Squadron & GC 1/145). Despite rather unjust opinion about struggling to convert to British (modern) aircraft, the Polish pilots, who previously flew Morane MS. 406s or Caudron Cyclones, had their Hawker Hurricane initiation rather similar to the homeboys. Sqn Ldr John A. Davis (British Commander) was killed after colliding with barrage balloons only two days after receiving Hurricanes; on the same day Flight Commander Flt Lt John Young landed with the wheels up. On 23 October 1940 Sqn Ldr Brenus Morris made an emergency landing too. Note Hurricane I ZF-U in the background.

The only Sqn 308 Hawker Hurricane I that can be traced so far is V6961 ZF-J, pictured here with Flg Off Jerzy Wolski and the squadron's mascot, 'Jumbie'. Wolski was killed in a flying accident on 11 January 1941 in a Miles Master.[27]

Unfortunately the only marking elements of the Hurricane in this photo of Sgt Władysław Majchrzyk and ground crew members that can be seen are two characters ,'V7' of the serial number, as well as application of the PAF chequer, below the cockpit, in the middle of the fuselage height. Majchrzyk flew with Sqn Ldr Davis and witnessed his death. 'City of Cracow' Squadron converted to Spitfire Is in April 1941.

Supermarine Spitfire IIA P7919 ZF-Y photographed in June 1941. The individual code letter 'Y' was extended to female name 'Ywonia', diminutive of Polish Iwona (Yvonne). This is the first documented case of PAF aircraft adorned this way!

Another Mk II Spitfire that was flown by No. 308 Sqn. IIA P8661 ZF-W was captured during AVM Trafford Leigh-Mallory's visit to RAF Northolt. Here AOC of No. 11 Group decorates Flg Off Witold Łokuciewski with the DFC. Flg Off Feliks Szyszka scored twice while flying this aircraft: one Bf 109 destroyed on 8 July 1941 and another probably destroyed the day before, and all of these only a week before this photo was taken.

At the beginning of September 1941, No. 308 Sqn started flying Spitfire Vs and suffering its first loss of a pilot killed on a new type, when Plt Off Czesław Budzałek flying Spitfire VB W3524 on 17 September 1941 collided in the air with a Bf 109 from 8./JG 26. On 28 October 1941, Gen. Władysław Sikorski visited Northolt, where No. 308 Sqn had operated since June 1941 and several photos were taken. Here VB AA735 ZF-N can be seen in the background, an aircraft usually flown by Flg Off Feliks Szyszka.

Flt Lt Stefan Janus, A Flight Commander (standing in the middle), had five of his claims reported when flying Spitfire IIBs and VBs[28] of No. 308 Sqn. On his right, Flg Off Franciszek Gomuliński, Technical Officer. The aircraft in the background is Spitfire VB AA735 which seems to be ZF-U now.

Sgt Tadeusz Schiele photographed with his Spitfire VB AB968 ZF-H in the autumn of 1941. Note the large PAF markings and pilot's emblem of The Big Dipper. In this case an individual code letter 'H' referred to Warsaw based 'Habarbusch & Schiele' brewery.

The same Sgt Schiele posing next to Spitfire VB AD330 in which he flew twice in operations in late 1941: on 23 November during 'Ramrod 12' and on 8 December when performing a sweep over France. This was the last operational sortie for No. 308 Sqn before moving to RAF Woodvale and leaving their Spitfire Vs to No. 316 Sqn. AD330 arrived in No. 308 Sqn right before Schiele's AB968 went off duty, therefore it was probably coded ZF-H. When 'City of Cracow' men were converting back to Mk Is and MK IIs, AD330 coded as SZ-H flew across the Channel, where it was shot down on 28 February 1942. Flg Off Józef Górski baled out and presumably drowned.[29]

Another example of 1941 or 1942 Spitfire VB from No. 308 Sqn adorned with a personal motif, although the identity of the aircraft is unknown.

RAF Northolt, Flt Lt Bernard Krupa, No. 316 Squadron's Adjutant, is reporting to Sqn Ldr Aleksander Gabszewicz on Squadron's Day (first anniversary of No. 316 Sqn formation) on 22 February 1942. Spitfire VB BL545 ZF-Q can be seen in the distance. Sqn Ldr Tadeusz Nowierski flew this aircraft from RAF Woodvale to RAF Northolt on 14 February 1942 to visit his former unit.

Flg Off Bruno Kudrewicz photographed in the first half of 1942, after the sortie, posing with the ground crew members and unidentified Spitfire VB (probably BL436 that he flew regularly) adorned with the large red and white (or actually white and red) chequer. Since the spring of 1942, soon after this photo was taken, PAF markings were applied in smaller size aft of the propeller.

Spitfire VB BL940 ZF-V was delivered to No. 308 Sqn at the end of June 1942 and flown during the Dieppe Raid only once, piloted by Flg Sgt Władysław Majchrzyk. On 3 February 1943 Sqn Ldr Walerian Żak was credited with one FW 190 probably destroyed while flying this aircraft.

A series of photos that depict an interesting emblem applied on 308's Spitfire VB. EN800 arrived in June 1942, when the bigger size of PAF colours were still in use; ZF-R code letters were applied. It is not certain whether 'a white cat with a small heart' emblem came with the aircraft or it was Polish creativity and invention. The new addition of a squadron badge of an arrow pointing towards the aircraft nose inside of a black diamond[30] can be seen in a photo of Flg Off Michał Najbicz sitting in a cockpit, as well as in a group photo taken at RAF Church Fenton in June 1943, where the entire B Flight pilots are posing with Sqn Ldr Józef Żulikowski, who is sitting in the middle.

No. 315 'CITY OF DĘBLIN' SQUADRON[31]

No. 315 'City of Dęblin' Squadron was formed on 21 January 1941 at RAF Acklington. Unlike some of the Polish fighter squadrons named after cities in Poland, where before the war Air Regiments were based[32], No. 315 paid their tribute to the small town of Dęblin, where No. 1 Air Force Training Centre was located. Their emblem of a fighting black rooster (used by 112th Fighter Squadron in Warsaw before the outbreak of war[33]) started to appear in the second half of 1942. Hawker Hurricane Is were used until the middle of July 1941, when the squadron moved to RAF Northolt. P2827 PK-K pictured here was regularly flown until 7 July 1941 when Plt Off Jerzy Czerniak wrecked it at RAF Speke. Sitting first from right is LAC Jan Kawa.

Sqn Ldr Stanisław Pietraszkiewicz, called 'Petro', posing next to his Hawker Hurricane I V7538 PK-O, that was previously flown during the Battle of Britain and used by No. 249 Sqn RAF. Note V7192 PK-U in the background.

On 13 March 1941, No. 315 Sqn arrived at RAF Speke continuing their operations on Hurricanes. Three shots of P3112 PK-A, the second aircraft the unit was equipped with, and remained with No. 315 Sqn for the whole duration of Hurricane usage. The aircraft was previously flown by No. 32 Sqn RAF. In July 1941 P3112 was left for No. 303 Sqn, which replaced No. 315 Sqn at Speke and was first flown on 17 July 1941 by Sqn Ldr Jerzy Jankiewicz.

Hawker Hurricane I P3835 PK-E came from No. 245 Sqn RAF almost at the same time as Flt Lt Władysław Szcześniewski, who previously served in this unit, and it was taken for its first (test) flight on 21 March 1941 by Plt Off Włodzimierz Miksa. This Hurricane performed its last operational sortie on 11 July 1941 when Plt Off Józef Czachowski flew a convoy patrol. Six days later, after being transferred to No. 303 Sqn, took off from Speke piloted by Flg Off Wojciech Kołaczkowski.

A group of mechanics proudly posing with their beloved 'pupil' Hawker Hurricane I V7003 PK-H.

Hawker Hurricane I R4200 was one of five aeroplanes of that type that arrived from Middle Wallop's based No. 32 Sqn RAF on 23 February 1941. Upon transition it was coded B and remained in No. 315 Sqn until conversion onto Spitfires.

No. 315 Sqn used No. 457 Sqn RAAF's Spitfire Is for conversion training, before receiving their own Mk IIAs from No. 308 Sqn, after joining Polish Wing at Northolt on 13 July 1941. One of these aircraft can be seen in this photo. Having a long career in No. 65 Sqn RAF (hence 'East India Squadron' emblem still visible under the cockpit) P7855 was delivered to No. 308 Sqn and coded ZF-B. Note an individual code letter 'K' extended to 'Krysia', a diminutive of Krystyna (Christine). 'Krysia' was damaged on 10 August 1941 when Sgt Aleksander Chudek crashed it on landing.

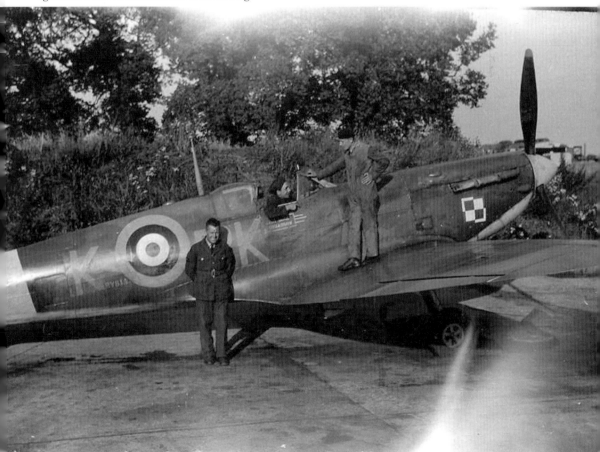

A reminder of the previous user: a large PAF chequer on this Spitfire cowling. Spitfire IIA P8387 also was former No. 308 Sqn aircraft and on being transferred to No. 315 Sqn it received code PK-H, with the letter H extend to 'HALINA', Polish female name. This aircraft was replaced by Spitfire IIB P8696 that was lost on 9 August 1941 together with its pilot Sgt Andrzej Niewiara.

Lady Virginia Child-Villiers, Countess of Jersey, known to be Charlie Chaplin's co-star in the 1931 *City Lights34*, but also as No. 315 Sqn's Mother, called 'Mummy', who visited her boys at RAF Woodvale in the summer of 1941. First from right is Sqn Ldr Stanisław Pietraszkiewicz, who was soon to be shot down and taken prisoner during Circus 101 in September 1941. Spitfire IIA, most probably 'Petro's' P8563 PK-E can be seen in this photo with Plt Off Władysław Grudziński (KIA on November 23, 1941) sitting in the cockpit. First from left is Flg Off Jan Falkowski, second Flt Lt Walerian Jasionowski, both unit pilots. P8563 was flown till end of August 1941 when, at the same time, another PK-E (IIB P8666) was in use and it was not an isolated situation.[35] After the war Lady Jersey married Polish fighter pilot Florian Martini and immigrated to the USA.

Spitfire IIB P8527 PK-A being refuelled. Sgt Tadeusz Krieger flew this aircraft on 14 August 1941 when he was credited with the destruction of a Bf 109 over Ardres.

The last days of August 1941 saw the arrival of Supermarine Spitfire Mk Vs, while No. 315 Sqn operated from RAF Northolt. This picture shows the first Mk V to be lost. Sgt Tadeusz Krieger was nearly killed when his Spitfire AB820 PK-M caught fire immediately after he started the engine.

From left to right are: Flg Offs Ignacy Olszewski, Michał Najbicz, Jan Falkowski, unk., Plt Off Władysław Zając, Sgts Jan Lipiński, Zygmunt Gruszczyński, Mieczysław Matus and Jacek Cieżowski. Spitfire in the background is AD134 PK-K that was used by two squadron NCOs to claim their victories. Sgt Stanisław Blok destroyed a Bf 109 and another Bf 109 probably destroyed on September 21, 1941. Exactly a month later Sgt Aleksander Chudek downed a FW 190.

Spitfire VB AB789 PK-R being maintained by the ground crew, including cleaning its 20 mm cannons. This aircraft was damaged on 23 November 1941 while piloted by Flg Off Olszewski when No. 315 Sqn lost five pilots killed and one wounded.

A group of pilots and a ground crew members are posing for the souvenir photo with the brand new Spitfire VB W3986 PK-F that was delivered in September 1941. From L – R are: Flg Off Zygmunt Drybański, Sgt Stanisław Blok, Sgt Mieczysław Matus, unknown, unkown, Sgt Aleksander Chudek, Flg Off Franciszek Kornicki and Flg Off Jan Falkowski. This aircraft was lost on 23 November 1941 during 'Ramrod 12' and Flg Off Władysław Grudziński was killed.

The first claim since conversion was made by Sgt Michał Cwynar on 16 September 1941. He scored the probable destruction of a Bf 109 flying Spitfire VB AB914 PK-Z, probably pictured here. From left to right standing are: Plt Off Józef Gil, Flt Lt Zbigniew Czaykowski, who reported Bf 109 shot down on the same sortie, Sgt Michał Cwynar, Plt Off Marian Łukaszewicz, Flg Off Henryk Stefankiewicz, Plt Off Tadeusz Andersz and Sgt Edward Jaworski. This aircraft, as the rest of Mk Vs, was later flown by No. 317 'City of Wilno' Squadron, after both units exchanged their aircraft.

VB W3328 PK-T was directly hit by German flak while performing an operational sortie on 21 October 1941.

The aircraft was piloted by Sgt Edward Jaworski, who shows the scale of the damage. Jaworski survived the war.

Sgt Tadeusz Krieger photographed in Spitfire VB AD134 PK-K. This aircraft was used on 21 September 1941 to claim one Bf 109 destroyed and another probably destroyed by Sgt Stanisław Blok, and on 21 October 1941 one FW 190 destroyed by Sgt Aleksander Chudek. Krieger was killed in a flying accident on 17 March 1942; AD134 was shot down on 1 May 1942 while in No. 242 Sqn RCAF and lost with Plt Off John Randolph Patton.

Two of 'City of Dęblin' Squadron pilots: Plt Off Władysław Grudziński and Sgt Stanisław Blok posing with Spitfire AB931 PK-C usually flown by Flg Off Włodzimierz Miksa. Miksa scored a triple success on 21 October 1941 claiming the destruction, probable destruction and damage of Bf 109s, while flying this mount. On 8 December 1941 Sqn Ldr Stefan Janus flew this Spitfire, when he shot down a Bf 109 over the Channel. Note a dwarf motif applied on both sides.

Two ground crew members photographed with the tail unit of Spitfire VB AA943 PK-F. This aircraft was flown by No. 315 Sqn between December 1941 and September 1942.

Photo taken at RAF Woodvale, where No. 315 Sqn rested between 1 April and 5 September 1942. Spitfire VB BM597 PK-C photographed here with two ground crew members, including LAC Stanisław Bączkiewicz (right), was later used by No. 317 Sqn as JH-C. BM597, owned by the Historical Aircraft Collection is still airworthy today, and can be seen during air shows across Europe, as well as at its base at Hangar 3, IWM, Duxford.

Plt Off Lech Kondracki flew with various Polish units, including No. 315 Sqn, where he was posted in June 1942. At the time when the whole batch of Spitfire Vs were exchanged with No. 317 Sqn, Kondracki also followed his posting to 'City of Wilno' Squadron. Since January 1943 he flew with No. 316 Sqn and he was killed over France on 9 August 1943, after colliding with his colleague Flg Off Michał Maciejowski. The latter survived the clash and spent the rest of the war as a PoW. Here, Kondracki poses with BM597, while BL544 PK-N can be seen in the background.

Supermarine Spitfire VB EN856 PK- B photographed in the summer of 1942. This was a brand new aircraft delivered to No. 315 Sqn, later handed over to No. 317 Sqn. The third Polish unit using this Spitfire was No. 303 Sqn.[36] While at RAF Ballyhalbert, on 14 December 1943 Flg Off Stanisław Podobiński flew this aircraft with the code RF-B and crashed into Rheast hill on the Isle of Man, losing his life.[37]

Spitfire VB W3764 PK-K was photographed at RAF Woodvale. This aircraft was damaged in a flying accident when its engine cut out and the aircraft hit a tree on 16 June 1942. Sgt Tadeusz Jankowski was wounded. Soon after a new PK-K arrived, it was BL238.

Flg Off Bolesław Sawiak poses with Mk V PK-I which presumably is EN840 delivered in June 1942. Note an individual letter 'I' below the propeller fading off.

On 12 July 1942 Spitfire VB AD230 PK-M was involved in collision with BM408 PK-X.

During an operational tour at RAF Northolt No. 315 Sqn lost 11 pilots killed in action and one in a flying accident, 3 pilots became PoWs and a further 7 were wounded. Despite claiming 28 E/A destroyed, 14 probably destroyed and 7 damaged, these men definitely needed time to rest. While taking a break at RAF Woodvale and commanded by Sqn Ldr Mieczysław Wiórkiewicz, a few encounters with the Luftwaffe took place. On 3 May 1942 Plt Off Konrad Stembrowicz shared the destruction of a Ju 88; then on 14 August 1942 Sgt Jerzy Malec damaged another aircraft of the same type. Nine days later Flg Off Bolesław Sawiak took off, despite his Section mate Sgt Tadeusz Lubicz-Lisowski's initial trouble and delay. Flying a lone patrol Sawiak spotted and immediately attacked a Ju 88 4U+KH from 1.(F)/123. Unfortunately his Spitfire VB BL959 PK-T was also hit by return fire and crash-landed at Fairgreen, near Ratoath in Ireland. The Polish pilot died of wounds in a local hospital, while the crew of the Ju 88, which also crash-landed, was interned.

No. 316 'CITY OF WARSAW' SQUADRON

No. 316 'City of Warsaw' Sqn was formed, as the seventh PAF fighter unit, on 23 February 1941 at RAF Pembrey and started getting in shape under the command of Sqn Ldr Juliusz Frey. A month later the Poles began with flying convoy patrols, but had to wait until 1 April 1941 when the Section led by Flg Off Aleksander Gabszewicz, who was called 'Count Oleś', attacked and downed an He 111 1G+LH from 1./KG 27, making this squadron's first victory. Gabszewicz's wingman Plt Off Bohdan Anders on that day flew Hawker Hurricane I V6635 SZ-X (pictured here before being delivered to No. 249 Sqn RAF, where it was flown, among others, by Sgt Michał Maciejowski, and then to No. 316 Sqn). It wasn't Gabszewicz's first Heinkel as he shot down one over Poland in 1939 and another over France in 1940. It has been said that Anders destroyed an He 111 over Poland too, however this claim was never approved. The latter was killed in a flying accident two months later, Gabszewicz on the other hand, rose to prominent rank within PAF.

Training on Hurricanes was not always an enjoyable experience. On 17 May 1941 Flt Lt Wacław Wilczewski barely survived one of those occasions when an engine of his W9231 SZ-L broke, while performing aerobatics. How the pilot left the wreckage without injuries remains a mystery.

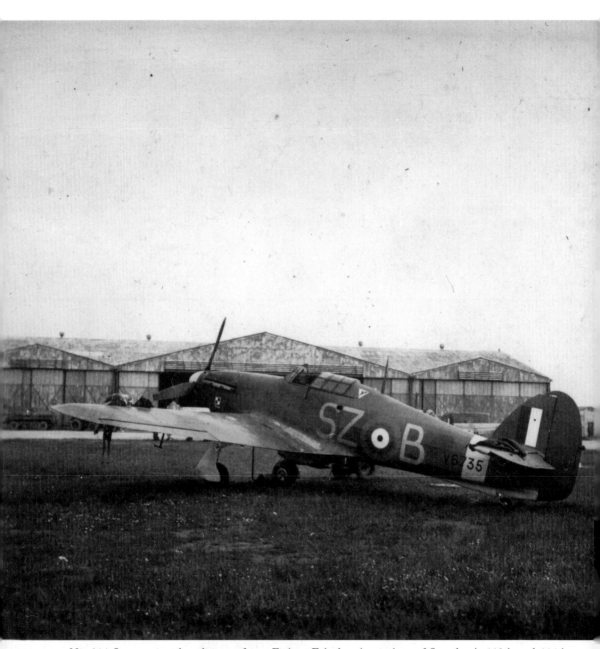

No. 316 Sqn continued traditions of two Fighter Eskadras (equivalent of Squadron): 113th and 114th of the IV/1 Dywizjon Myśliwski (equivalent of Fighter Wing) in Warsaw, hence discussion took place which of the two unit's badges should be applied in Britain. Finally the flying owl of the 113th Fighter Squadron was chosen, although for some time 'City of Warsaw' B Flight aircraft were adorned with 114th Fighter Squadron's flying swallow to show that the initial crew consisted of former members of both units. Hurricane I V6735 SZ-B photographed at RAF Pembrey was first flown by Plt Off Zbigniew Nosowicz on 24 February 1941. It had been used before by No. 302 Sqn during the Battle of Britain as WX-M. Note the application of the squadron's emblem aft of the cockpit canopy, and PAF colours below the exhaust.

V6958 SZ-D operated from the beginning of No. 316 Sqn's service and it was last flown on 16 June 1941 by Plt Off Franciszek Kozłowski.

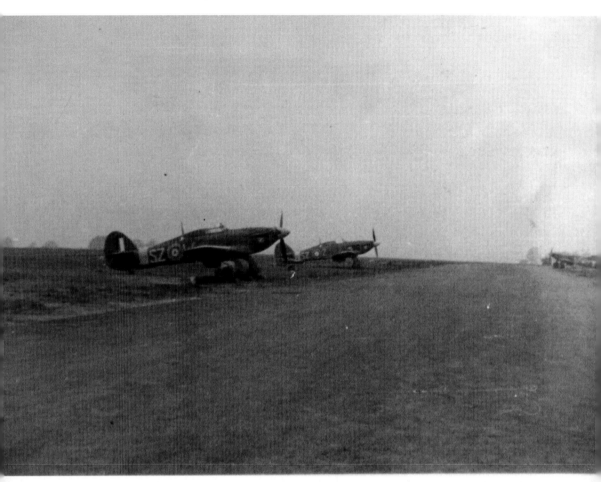

June 1941 saw No. 316 Sqn converting to Hawker Hurricane IIAs and IIBs. B Flight's IIAs were photographed at RAF Church Stanton, where this unit moved on 2 August 1941 after their time at RAF Colerne. These are Z2751 SZ-W, Z2774 SZ-Z and Z2962 SZ-T (or Z2750 SZ-Y) in the distance. The latter, piloted by Flg Off Marian Szawlewicz, was involved in a mid-air collision on 28 August 1941 with another Hurricane IIB Z3586 SZ-V. Szawlewicz was wounded, but his colleague Flg Off Dariusz Gozdecki lost his life.

Hurricane IIA Z2565 SZ-R of B Flight adorned with the emblem that looks like a flying swallow. This aircraft was first tested on 20 June 1941 by Flt Lt Wacław Wilczewski (as first Mk II flown by No. 316 Sqn airman) and four days later sent for convoy patrol piloted by Sgt Paweł Gallus. Since then it was used until conversion to Spitfire Vs.

Caught in the act: Hurricane II Z2462 SZ-O with the clear view of Polish national marking and POLAND underneath. The empty triangle applied in the typical way for a swallow emblem is noteworthy too. Is it either not yet complete or someone interrupted its application. Using squadron artwork other than what was agreed would not be an isolated case. No. 303 Sqn B Flight pilots during Battle of Britain painted a winged salamander motif on pilot's hut's doors to say: we may fly and die together, but our origins are in two different units: 111th ('Kościuszko' badge) and 112th (Winged Salamander badge[38])! And, again, it was Flt Lt Wilczewski flying this mount for the first time on 21 June 1941.

Finally, on 15 October 1941, No. 316 Sqn received their Spitfire Vs as the second squadron of the No. 2 Polish Wing, created on 18 August 1941 at RAF Exeter.[39] Plt Off Tadeusz Dobrut-Dobrucki, KIA on 28 February 1942, poses with the ground crew members with an ex No. 308 Sqn mount AD363 SZ-R adorned with the flying swallow emblem. Dobrucki flew his final mission in this Spitfire.

Sqn Ldr Aleksander Gabszewicz and his personal Spitfire VB P8606 SZ-G (one of many 'Gs' that he flew during his career in the West) that he flew at the beginning of 1942. This aircraft was funded by Lady Doreen Hope from New Delhi and adorned with the name of 'DELHI II' on the fuselage. Gabszewicz damaged one FW 190 on 27 March 1942 while flying this Spitfire. P8606 was flown by Flg Off Jan Muszel on 4 April 1942 during 'Circus 119', when both were lost close to the French Coast.

There is no question that this VB AA858 SZ-D belonged to the A Flight as the Flying Owl is clearly visible. This aircraft later flew with two Polish fighter squadrons, Nos. 306 and 302.

Flg Off Bernard Buchwald flew Spitfire VB AD130 SZ-E on 12 April 1942 when he experienced engine failure. Even worse, all this happened while engaging with FW 190s over France. Buchwald spent the rest of the war as a PoW.

Spitfire VBs of No. 316 Sqn captured while taking off from RAF Northolt in early 1942. Among them is BL646 SZ-R named 'Muntok' after Dutch East Indies town. This was a personal mount of Flt Lt Stanisław Skalski, at that time B Flight Commander. Apart from 'Curly', as Skalski was rather ironically called due to the first signs of hair loss, who reported destruction of a FW 190 on 10 April and the probable destruction of another E/A of the same type on 3 May both in 1942. It was also a lucky plane for Sgt Władysław Kiedrzyński to claim a FW 190 downed two days after Skalski's last triumph. Furthermore Plt Off Mieczysław Wyszkowski probably destroyed a FW 190 on 3 June 1942 flying it. In the second photo 'Ryś', squadron's mascot, poses with BL646.

Spitfire VB AR434 SZ-J delivered to No. 316 Sqn in June 1942. It later served with another Polish squadron, No. 315. This aircraft has a puzzling emblem on its rudder as well as unknown personal motif below the windscreen.

No. 317 'CITY OF WILNO' SQUADRON

Hawker Hurricane I V7013 JH-L from No. 317 'City of Wilno' Squadron, the last day fighter PAF unit that was organised on 20 February 1941 at RAF Acklington and, similarly to Nos. 302 and 308, operated only Hurricanes and Spitfires until its disbandment. Picture was taken at RAF Ouston. Note unpainted cockpit hood.

The same aircraft photographed with the ground crew, Plt Off Stanisław Bochniak, also known as 'Żaba' (Frog), who is playing an accordion, and squadron's mascot, dog 'Lipa'.

When formed, No. 317 Sqn was commanded by Sqn Ldr Stanisław Brzezina, and his right hand and friend Flt Lt Henryk Szczęsny (standing in the middle) initially took Flight B. They had known each other since the early days in Poland, when Brzezina was in charge of fighter training, and Szczęsny was one of his trusted instructors. They both fought in the Battle of Britain, posted to No. 74 Sqn (which coincidentally used JH code before the war) and were known as 'Breezy' and 'Sneezy'. The latter was also known as 'Henry the Pole ' or 'Hesio' (diminutive of Polish Henryk) and this was his 'trade mark' while in No. 317 Sqn. Note his nickname above the PAF chequer applied on his personal Mk I W3972 JH-S. Szczęsny claimed two shared victories when flying this mount, on 10 and 14 July 1941, both with Sgt Stanisław Brzeski. Flg Off Paweł Niemiec is having fun on the starboard wing. The latter shared victory of a Ju 88 with Sgt Tadeusz Baranowski on 2 June 1941, claiming No. 317's first kill.

When claiming his Ju 88 together with Szczęsny on 14 July 1941, Sgt Stanisław Brzeski flew Mk I V6565 JH-U, photographed at RAF Fairwood Common. T9520 JH-T and V7339 JH-X (damaged by Sgt Jan Malinowski on 1 July 1941) can be seen in the background.

The same Hurricane I V7339 JH-X. This aircraft participated in two 'Gudgeon' operations, the first on 10 July 1941 when piloted by Sgt Brzeski, who shared a Bf 109 (and the last 317's claim on in a Hurricane); and the second on 14 July 1941 when flown by Flg Off Tadeusz Koc. Gudgeons were No. 317 Sqn first full scale sorties after countless patrols flown in sections only.

The middle of July 1941 saw the arrival of Hurricane IIAs and IIBs. In this picture No. 317 Sqn pilots are posing with IIB Z3502 JH-J, previously used in No. 306 Sqn. From left standing are: Plt Off Tadeusz Szulc, Plt Off Tadeusz Kratke, Wg Cdr Stanisław Brzezina (Commander of No. 2 Polish Wing at Exeter, killed in a flying accident on 13 February 1946 while in BAFO), Sqn Ldr Henryk Szczęsny (now leading the squadron) and Sgt Bronisław Kościk (killed on 7 March 1942 while returning from a sortie). Note that the PAF colours are re-positioned on the cowling.

Hurricane II JH-Q (serial number unknown) with the B Flight pilots. Flt Lt Piotr Ozyra, B Flight Commander, is standing under the propeller. He was killed on 29 April 1942 while commanding No. 317 Sqn.

Plt Off Karol Wójcik poses in front of Hawker Hurricane IIA Z3559 JH-H. This aircraft was previously used by No. 306 Sqn as UZ-P, then transferred to No. 317 Sqn and flown between July and October 1941. Later Z3559 was delivered to No. 312 (Czechoslovak) Sqn. Wójcik failed to return from an operational sortie on 29 November 1941 while in Spitfire VB W3968.

Sqn Ldr Szczęsny's new mount, Z3975 JH-S. The application and style have changed, but 'Hesio' leaves no doubt who flew it. Note the two swastikas under the exhaust.

Miraculously Sgt Jan Malinowski, who piloted this Hurricane IIA Z3587 JH-T, survived. Photo shows what was left after the aircraft hit a tree on approach to RAF Exeter on 29 August 1941.

In October 1941 all three squadrons, Nos. 302, 316 and 317 converted to Spitfire Vs, including AD308 JH-T photographed with Flg Off Tadeusz Koc. On 15 February 1942, Flg Sgt Stanisław Brzeski mistook Liberator AM918 as enemy aeroplane and shot it down together with Sgt Jan Malinowski, while flying AD308.

Sqn Ldr Henryk Szczęsny's new personal aircraft, Spitfire VB AD350 JH-S. Note squadron's emblem of a flying condor that goes back to 151st and 152nd Fighter Squadrons of III/V Fighter Wing in Wilno, both based at Lida aerodrome. It was designed by Sub. Lt. Anatol Piotrowski, a pilot killed in action the very first day of the Polish Campaign. Since late 1941 it was applied aft of the cockpit. Before No. 317 Sqn command was handed over to Sqn Ldr Józef Brzeziński, Szczęsny had one more JH-S, BL543 also adorned with his nickname.

Sqn Ldr Szczęsny poses in AD350. Note that he is wearing a 'Tiger' Mae West, reminiscent of his days in No. 74 Sqn.

Flg Off Roman Hrycak and visitors from the Polish Navy are photographed with Spitfire AA762 JH-W adorned with two swastikas. These most probably are the symbols of Flg Sgt Michał Maciejowski's victories reported on 30 December 1941. He shot down two Bf 109s on that day while flying this aircraft.

Spitfire VB W3970 JH-Y photographed in early 1942. Note the small diameter of the RAF roundel applied on a limited number of aircraft only.

Spitfire VB AD140 JH-H photographed in rather idyllic scenery. This aircraft was flown by Flt Lt Józef Brzeziński on 18 December 1941 when he claimed the destruction of a Bf 109. AD140 was damaged on 15 March 1942 during No. 317's Black Day. After an uneventful mission the pilots tried to land at Bolt Head. Due to bad weather conditions nine of them crash landed, four were injured, while Sqn Ldr Józef Brzeziński (appointed two weeks prior the tragedy) hit the cliff in his BL805 JH-N and was killed. One of the wounded pilots was Flg Off Tadeusz Kratke, who flew AD140 JH-H on that day. The aircraft was written off.

A personal Spitfire VB of Flg Off Stanisław Bochniak adorned with his pre-war sweetheart's name 'Hala'. This is presumably AD269 JH-B that was used four times during aerial cover of the Dieppe assault by Sgts Kazimierz Sztramko, Adam Kolczyński (two sorties, he shared destruction of a Do 217) and Plt Off Tadeusz Felc.

Flg Off Tadeusz Kratke photographed with Spitfire VB BL627 JH-H with the word 'Mała' (a Little One, which was probably how one of the squadron pilots addressed his girlfriend) that replaced presentation name of 'WONOSOBO'. 'Mała' is hardly visible above pilot's head. Kratke frequently flew BL627 between May and July 1942, damaging a few Bf 109s parked at Offrethun on 24 July. Seven days later he was shot down over the Channel while flying this aircraft, baled out and was picked up after two hours spent in a dinghy. Note the new way of how the squadron badge had been applied: the diamond shaped background has gone and the location has changed.

A group of ground crew members pose for a souvenir photo with a Spitfire VB BL860 JH-T at RAF Northolt. This would be Bochniak's new mount with the name of 'Hala' yet to be applied.

… and there they are, Stanisław Bochniak and 'Hala' (little Halina, Bochniak's pre-war girlfriend). This aircraft was flown during the Dieppe Raid by Sqn Ldr Tadeusz Nowierski, Deputy Wing Commander, when he claimed two Do 217s damaged. During later sorties on 19 August 1942, Wg Cdr Tadeusz Rolski flew BL860 twice, but made no claims.

Personal Spitfire VB AA758 JH-V of Sqn Ldr Piotr Ozyra adorned with his nickname 'Bazyli Kwiek'. Ozyra was shot down and killed on 29 April 1942. Three months later, on 24 July 1942, Flg Off Witold Łanowski, pictured here, flew this aircraft during Rhubarb operation and was hit by AA.

Despite quite substantial damage Łanowski managed to return to RAF Northolt. Here the results of shrapnel hit are being inspected by Flt Lt Kazimierz Rutkowski, No. 317 Sqn B Flight Commander, Wg Cdr Stefan Janus, who led No. 1 Polish Wing and Sqn Ldr Tadeusz Nowierski, Deputy Commander of the Wing. Two days later Janus claimed his last, out of six, victories and on 19 August 1942 he took the whole Wing over Dieppe. During Operation 'Jubilee' Rutkowski downed a Do 217 and a He 111 while Nowierski damaged two Do 217s. On that day AA758 was piloted by Sgt Władysław Pawłowski, when he damaged a FW 190, but was also badly damaged.

Sqn Ldr Stanisław Skalski commanded No. 317 Sqn after Ozyra's death. Here he is photographed with his Spitfire VB BM131 JH-Q. During the Dieppe Raid he flew this mount three times. Plt Off Bochniak also piloted this aircraft once during an uneventful mission on that day.

The same BM131 JH-Q photographed two months earlier, on 14 June 1942 on American Flag Day.

'City of Wilno' only victim during Operation 'Jubilee' was Flg Off Marian Cholewka, who was badly wounded (Spitfire AR340 JH-P). Here he is sitting on Spitfire VB BL690 JH-Z's wing. This aircraft brought luck to Flt Lt Rutkowski on that day. EN919 JH-N, visible in the background, was damaged on 7 July 1942 when Sgt Piotr Kuryłłowicz landed at Northolt.

19 August 1942 at RAF Northolt. One of 'Jubilee's victorious pilots, Flt Lt Kazimierz Rutkowski, looks happy after scoring one Do 217 and one He 111, both destroyed. Spitfires visible in the distance are BL860 JH-T (left) flown on that day by Wg Cdr Tadeusz Rolski Senior Operations Officer from HQ No. 11 Group; BM566 JH-S (right) was flown by Plt Off Stanisław Brzeski to claim the destruction of a He 111.

Chapter 5

Poles in RAF Squadrons

To cover the Polish pilots serving in RAF Squadrons would require a separate book. It would not be possible to explore all the cases in a small chapter, hence only a few examples will be shown here. After the Battle of Britain many of them remained in their units for some time, before being posted to PAF squadrons. Meanwhile new pilots started to arrive, being posted to Polish as well as to RAF squadrons. In the latter case they needed to get to know new equipment, to understand British tactics and to learn the language of Islanders. Sgts Józef Biel and Paweł Gallus are photographed with the Hawker Hurricane I, while with No. 3 Sqn at RAF Castletown. After a short stay in No. 303 Sqn Gallus was posted to No. 3 Sqn on 27 September 1940, where he was joined by Biel in October, and both served there until February 1941, then receiving postings to Nos. 316 Sqn and 317 Sqn respectively.

Flg Off Władysław Szulkowski, first from left, was another Battle of Britain veteran who made a lot of friends while serving in No. 65 Sqn RAF. He was probably happy when posting to the newly formed No. 315 Sqn came through, but sad leaving his mates behind. From flying Spitfires with the British to Hurricanes in 'City of Dęblin', he would eventually be killed in a Hurricane I.

Plt Off Bolesław Drobiński was another Pole flying with No. 65 Sqn during the Battle of Britain and extending his stay in this unit. Here, he is photographed in the cockpit of Spitfire I X4820 YT-B usually flown by Plt Off Ron Wigg, who is standing in the foreground. Drobiński flew this aircraft in January 1941.

Flg Off Jan Falkowski flew Hurricanes while in No. 32 Sqn RAF, which he joined on 12 October 1940. On 16 January 1941 he shot down a He 111, but his Hurricane II Z2984 was also hit. The Pole baled out and broke a leg.

This picture of No. 85 Sqn RAF Hurricanes was probably taken on 18 October 1940. Plt Off Czesław Tarkowski flew Hurricane I V7240 VY-M, visible second from right. Eight days later he was posted to No. 605 Sqn RAF. Although he served in both during the Battle of Britain, he was a non-operational pilot by then.

No. 501 Sqn RAF Hawker Hurricane I V7650 SD-O with the inscription below the cockpit 'Secunderabad City' and the Polish pilot Sgt Romuald Gadus inside.

Spitfire I R6597 UM-V of No. 152 Sqn was flown by Sgt Józef Szlagowski on 28 November 1940.

On 9 November 1940, eight Polish fighter pilots were posted to RAF Aldergrove with No. 245 Sqn RAF. These men were: Flt Lts Stefan Łaszkiewicz, Jerzy Orzechowski, Władysław Szcześniewski, Flg Off Jan Wiśniewski, Plt Off Tadeusz Koc, Sgts Stanisław Brzeski, Bronisław Kościk and Franciszek Prętkiewicz. The latter was killed in a flying accident in Hawker Hurricane I R4079 DX-E on 30 November 1940, the others flew convoy patrols. In May 1941 another two pilots joined the squadron: Flg Off Zygmunt Bieńkowski and Plt Off Bolesław Palej. A formation of No. 245 Sqn Hurricane Is was photographed over Northern Ireland including P3101 DX-O that was occasionally flown by Flts Łaszkiewicz, Szcześniewski, Flg Off Wiśniewski, Sgts Kościk and Prętkiewicz; P3762 DX-F was used by Flt Lts Łaszkiewicz, Szcześniewski, Flg Off Wiśniewski, Plt Off Koc, Sgts Brzeski, Kościk and Prętkiewicz. Hurricane R4079 DX-E was once flown by Szcześniewski and it was the aircraft piloted by Prętkiewicz during his last tragic sortie.

Hawker Hurricane I V9241 DX-C that on 4 March 1941 was flown by Plt Off Koc and on 4 May 1941 by Flg Off Bieńkowski.

Plt Off Marian Łukaszewicz gained combat experience in Poland (while in 151st Fighter Squadron) and then in France (GC 1/145). In November 1940 he was posted to No. 616 Sqn RAF to fly Spitfire Is. He would not survive another year, losing his life on 23 November 1941 while in No. 315 Sqn.

Supermarine Spitfire IIA P7895 RN-N from No. 72 Sqn RAF. This aircraft was flown by two Polish pilots of this unit: Plt Off Tadeusz Stabrowski (KIA 11 March 1943 while in No. 308 Sqn) and Jerzy Godlewski (KIA 10 July 1941 while in No. 72 Sqn RAF).

Flg Off Warren Sandman poses next to Spitfire II P8261 ZP-N that was occasionally flown by Plt Off Stanisław Król, who served in No. 74 Sqn RAF. Król was shot down on 2 July 1941 (Spitfire VB W3263) and taken prisoner. After escaping from Stalag Luft III in Sagan he was captured and murdered by the Germans on 12 April 1944.

Flg Off Mieczysław Gorzula (third from left) photographed while in No. 87 Sqn RAF where he learnt night flying in Hurricane Is and IIs. He was another Polish pilot fighting in the Battle of Britain (Sqns.615 and 607), and then flew in No. 229 Sqn RAF, who extended his RAF connections. The aircraft behind is Hurricane IIA BE500 LK-A with the presentation name 'Cawnpore I', the personal mount of Sqn Ldr Denis Smallwood. It was flown in May 1942 by another Polish pilot Sgt Henryk Trybulec attached to 'United Provinces' Squadron.

Again, No. 87 Sqn and one more Polish pilot photographed at RAF Colerne in December 1941. Sgt Antoni Beda, standing seventh from left, fought in the Battle of Britain in No. 302 Sqn, then on 26 September 1941 was sent to No. 87 Sqn to polish his night flying skills. A month later he was involved in a mid-air collision with another Pole Sgt Paweł Gallus, but both survived. Apart from those mentioned, there were other Polish pilots flying with No. 87 Sqn: Flg Off Andrzej Malarowski, Flt Lt Jerzy Orzechowski, Sgt Bolesław Sochacki and Flg Off Antoni Waltoś.

Flg Off Malarowski photographed with Hawker Hurricane IIC HL864 LK-? 'Nightingale'. He flew many sorties in No. 87 Sqn's aircraft, but there is no evidence of the Pole ever piloting this one.

Douglas Havoc I BD112 YP-T of No. 23 Sqn RAF. Another unit where Polish fliers were posted (in May 1941). These men were: Flg Off Kazimierz Bokowiec, Plt Off Stefan Gębicki, Plt Off Stanisław Reymer-Krzywicki, Flg Off Władysław Różycki, Plt Off Edward Ryciak and Flg Off Andrzej Strasburger.[1] Out of these men only Różycki was a fighter pilot with combat experience gained in Poland and during the Battle of Britain; Reymer-Krzywicki was a bomber pilot, the others were navigators or radio-operators. Poles flew Douglas Havoc Is, including BD112 that was used to claim one Ju 88 destroyed and another damaged on 7 December 1941. Douglas Boston IIIs and Douglas Turbinlites were also flown by the Polish airmen in No. 85 Sqn RAF and No. 1454 Flight RAF respectively.

No. 92 'East India' Squadron Spitfire Vs photographed in the air. On 8 July 1941 Sgt Adolf Pietrasiak claimed his fourth Bf 109 flying R7195 QJ-B visible in this photo. In total he destroyed six Bf 109s and one shared while in No. 92 Sqn, mostly while in Spitfire W3245. Interestingly No. 92 Sqn was previously coded with GR letters, which in July 1940 were assigned to Polish No. 301 Sqn.

Plt Off Stanisław 'Charlie' Blok was one of many Poles who, during their operational career, had to accept every posting that allowed them to fly. He joined No. 56 Sqn RAF, and then transferred to No. 315 Sqn PAF, where he claimed three victories (including one probable). Then he was sent north to fly with Nos. 603, 54 and 164 Sqns RAF. While in No. 603 'City of Edinburgh' at RAF Peterhead he used Spitfire VB AD502 XT-Z occasionally. When in No. 164 Sqn, he was credited with the shared destruction of a Ju 88. Later Blok served with No. 315 Sqn again, No. 504 Sqn RAF and once more with No. 315, scoring three FW 190s destroyed and another two damaged.

In February 1942 a small group of Polish volunteers, mostly pilots unsuitable to fly in front line fighter squadrons, joined No. 112 'Flying Sharks' Sqn in Libya to fly Curtiss Kittyhawk Is. For the prize of only one shared victory, gained by Sgt Zbigniew Urbańczyk (standing left) and 140 operational sorties flown, achievements of the Polish group were rather unfavourable: two pilots were killed, two others wounded and they lost two aircraft. Sgt Jerzy Różański, photographed sitting on the wing of AK637 GA-I, and standing on right in the second photo, later joined No. 300 Sqn flying Lancasters. He was lost with the whole crew on 12/13 June 1944.

Sqn Ldr Jerzy Jankiewicz was the first Pole to command an RAF Squadron. On 22 May 1942 this officer became the leader of No. 222 Sqn, but sadly he was killed three days later, when leading North Weald Wing and piloting Spitfire VB AD233 ZD-F.

Hawker Hurricane IIs of No. 87 Sqn photographed in 1942. Although normally painted in Night Black, for the purpose of Operation 'Jubilee', the camouflage was changed to Ocean Grey and Dark Green, leaving No. 87 as the only night fighter squadron involved in aerial cover of the Dieppe Landing, applying such change. No. 43 Sqn sent their aircraft in Night Black. On that day Flg Off Andrzej Malarowski flew two sorties in Hurricane II Z2643 LK-J, seen in this photo. He was hit by ground fire and had to land at RAF Tangmere on the last drops of fuel, where he removed a bullet that penetrated the tank.[2] His colleague Flg Off Antoni Waltoś was killed on that day in Hurricane IIA Z2497 LK-X.[3] During his stay with No. 87 Sqn Malarowski also flew LK-C visible in this photo, while his colleague Sgt Henryk Trybulec piloted BE500 LK-A, LK-C, LK-E, Z2643 LK-J, BD833 LK-Q and LK-T.

Another photograph of No. 87 Sqn Hurricanes, including those flown by the Polish pilots: BE566 LK-Z (Malarowski and Trybulec lost on 25 April 1942 over a week after the photo was taken), BD833 LK-Q (Trybulec), BE513 or BE514 LK-F (Malarowski), Z3775 LK-B (Malarowski), BE500 LK-A (Trybulec) and BD952 LK-G (Malarowski).

Appendix I

Fighter Aircraft Flown by the Poles in Operations in France 1940

Morane Saulnier MS.406

So called 'Montpellier Group, divided into frontline sections: Cpt. Stefan Łaszkiewicz Section attached to GCIII/2; Cpt. Jan Pentz Section attached to GCII/6; Cpt. Mieczysław Sulerzycki Section attached to GCIII/6; Lt. Kazimierz Bursztyn Section attached to GCIII/1; Lt. Józef Brzeziński Section attached to GCI/2; Lt. Władysław Goettel Section attached to GCII/7[1]; Lt. Wojciech Januszewicz Frontline Fighter Section attached to GCII/7

DAT Sections: Maj. Zdzisław Krasnodębski Section attached to GCI/55; Lt. Franciszek Skiba Section attached to GCI/55; Cpt. Kazimierz Kuzian Section, Nantes; Cpt. Tadeusz Opulski Section, Romorantin; Lt. Czesław Sałkiewicz, Toulouse

Caudron Renault CR.714 Cyclone

GC1/145 'Varsovie' (the only Polish fighter squadron formed and sent to fight)

Marcel Bloch MB.151

GC1/145 'Varsovie'[2]

Frontline Sections: Maj. Edward Więckowski Section attached to GCIII/9; Lt. Ludwik Paszkiewicz Section attached to GCII/8

DAT Sections: Lt. Jan Falkowski Section, Cognac; Lt. Robert Janota Section, Angers; Cdt. Ryszard Budrewicz Section, Tours; Cpt. Adam Kowalczyk Section, La Rochelle; Lt. Zdzisław Henneberg Section, Châteauroux

Marcel Bloch MB.152

GC1/145 'Varsovie'; Maj. Zdzisław Krasnodębski Section attached to GCI/55
Frontline Fighter Sections: Cpt. Jan Pentz Section attached to GCII/6; Lt. Arsen Cebrzyński Section attached to GCII/6; Cpt. Franciszek Jastrzębski Section attached to GCII/1; Maj. Edward Więckowski Section attached to GCIII/9; Lt. Ludwik Paszkiewicz Section attached to GCII/8; Maj. Eugeniusz Wyrwicki Section attached to GCII/10; Lt. Aleksander Gabszewicz Section attached to GCIII/10

DAT Sections: Lt. Jan Falkowski Section, Cognac; Cdt. Ryszard Budrewicz Section, Tours; Cpt. Jan Kowalczyk Section, La Rochelle; Lt. Zdzisław Henneberg Section, Châteauroux; Lt. Mieczysław Wolański Group, Châteaudun; Maj. Zdzisław Krasnodębski Section, Châteaudun and Etampes

Kolhooven FK.58

Cpt. Walerian Jasionowski so called 'Kolhooven Flight'; Maj. Zdzisław Krasnodębski Section attached to GCI/55

Curtiss Hawk H.75

Cpt. Stefan Łaszkiewicz Section attached to GCIII/2

DAT Sections: Maj. Zdzisław Krasnodębski Section attached to GCI/55; Cpt. Bronisław Kosiński Section, Bourges

Dewoitine D.501 & D.510

Sub.Lt. Michał Kolubiński DAT Section, Rennes and Clermont-Ferrand; Cpt. Mieczysław Wiórkiewicz Training Fighter Flight, Mions; Cpt. Stanisław Pietraszkiewicz Group, Bordeaux/Bussac; Sub.Lt. Stanisław Andrzejewski Group, Cean

Dewoitine D.520

Lt. Władysław Goettel Section attached to GCII/7; Cpt. Mieczysław Sulerzycki Section attached to GCIII/6

Arsenal VG.33

Maj. Zdzisław Krasnodębski Section attached to GCI/55

Appendix II

Polish Fighter Units Formed Under British Command 1940–1941

NO. 302 'CITY OF POZNAŃ' SQUADRON[1]

Operated: formed 13 July 1940 at RAF Leconfield, disbanded 18 December 1946 at RAF Hethel.

Code letters: WX, from August 1945 QH.

Aircraft: Hurricane, Spitfire (see Appendix 1)

Bases: Leconfield from 13 July 1940 (including operating from Duxford), Northolt from 11 October 1940, Westhampnett from 23 November 1940, Kenley from 7 April 1941, Jurby from 28 May 1941 (including operating from Valley), Church Stanton from 7 August 1941, Warmwell from 5 September 1941, Harrowbeer from 5 October 1941, Ibsley from 25 October 1941, Harrowbeer from 5 November 1941, Warmwell from 26 April 1942, Heston from 7 May 1942, Croydon from 30 June 1942, Heston from 7 July 1942, Kirton-in-Lindsey from 1 February 1943 (including operating from Derby), Hutton Cranswick from 17 April 1943, Heston 1 June 1943, Perranporth from 20 June 1943, Fairlop from 19 August 1943, Tangmere from 18 September 1943, Northolt from 21 September 1943, Fairwood Common from 31 March 1944, Deanland from 1 April 1944, Southend from 12 April 1944, Deanland from 14 April 1944, Chailey from 26 April 1944, Appledram from 28 June 1944, Ford from 16 July 1944, Plumetôt B.10 from 3 August 1944, Lille/Vendeville B.51 from 16 September 1944, Antwerp/Deurne B.70 from 3 October 1944, St. Denijs Westrem B.61 from 11 October 1944, Grimbergen B.60 from 13 January 1945, Gilze Rijen B.77 from 8 March 1945, Nordhorn B.101 from 13 April 1945, Varrelbusch B.113 from 30 April 1945, Ahlhorn B.111 from 16 September 1945, Hethel from 7 October 1946.

Total score: 44½ enemy aircraft destroyed, 24 probably destroyed, 16 damaged.[2]

Losses (killed in operations and training): 27

Commanding Officers: Sqn Ldr Mieczysław Mümler from 13 July 1940, Sqn Ldr Piotr Łaguna from 7 December 1940, Sqn Ldr Stefan Witorzeńć from 29 May 1941, Sqn Ldr Julian Kowalski from 28 November 1941, Sqn Ldr Stanisław Łapka from 25 August 1942, Sqn Ldr Wieńczysław Barański from 16 May 1943, Sqn Ldr Wacław Król from 18 October 1943, Sqn Ldr Marian Duryasz from 7 July 1944, Sqn Ldr Zygmunt Bieńkowski from 1 January 1945 (PoW), Sqn Ldr Ignacy Olszewski from 24 February 1945 (SEC),[3] Sqn Ldr Bolesław Kaczmarek from 24 March 1945, Sqn Ldr Jerzy Szymankiewicz from 1 August 1945.

RAF Commander:[4] Sqn Ldr William A.J. Satchell from 13 July 1940 to 1 January 1941.

NO. 303 'TADEUSZ KOŚCIUSZKO.⁵ CITY OF WARSAW' SQUADRON

Operated: formed 2 August 1940 at RAF Northolt, disbanded 11 December 1946 at RAF Hethel.

Code letters: RF, from August 1945 PD.

Aircraft: Hurricane, Spitfire, Mustang

Bases: Northolt from 2 August 1940, Leconfield from 11 October 1940, Northolt from 3 January 1941, Speke from 13 July 1941, Northolt from 7 October 1941, Kirton-in-Lindsey from 15 June 1942, Redhill from 16 August 1942, Kirton-in-Lindsey from 20 August 1942, Northolt from 1 February 1943, Heston from 5 February 1943, Debden from 3 March 1943, Heston from 12 March 1943, Martlesham Heath from 26 March 1943, Heston from 8 April 1943, Northolt from 1 June 1943, Ballyhalbert from 12 November 1943, Horne from 30 April 1944, Westhampnett from 19 June 1944, Merston from 27 June 1944, Westhampnett from 9 August 1944, Coltishall from 25 September 1944, Andrews Field from 4 April 1945, Coltishall from 16 May 1945, Andrews Field from 9 August 1945, Turnhouse from 28 November 1945, Wick from 1 January 1946, Charterhall from 3 March 1946, Hethel from 23 March 1946.

Total score: 187 1/6 enemy aircraft destroyed, 35 probably destroyed and 22 damaged.⁶

Losses (killed in operations and training): 39 + 4 after the war

Commanding Officers: Sqn Ldr Zdzisław Krasnodębski from 2 August 1940, Sqn Ldr Witold Urbanowicz from 7 September 1940, Flg Off Zdzisław Henneberg from 22 October 1940, Sqn Ldr Adam Kowalczyk from 7 November 1940, Sqn Ldr Zdzisław Henneberg⁷ from 20 February 1941 (†), Flt Lt Tadeusz Arentowicz from 13 April 1941, Sqn Ldr Wacław Łapkowski from 5 May 1941 (†), Sqn Ldr Tadeusz Arentowicz from 3 July 1941 (†), Sqn Ldr Jerzy Jankiewicz from 9 July 1941, Sqn Ldr Wojciech Kołaczkowski from 21 November 1941, Sqn Ldr Walerian Żak from 7 May 1942, Sqn Ldr Jan Zumbach from 19 May 1942, Sqn Ldr Zygmunt Bieńkowski from 1 December 1942, Sqn Ldr Jan Falkowski from 4 July 1943, Sqn Ldr Tadeusz Koc from 21 November 1943, Sqn Ldr Bolesław Drobiński from 25 September 1944, Sqn Ldr Witold Łokuciewski from 1 February 1946.

RAF Commander: Sqn Ldr Ronald G. Kellett from 2 August 1940 to 1 January 1941.

NO. 306 'CITY OF TORUŃ' SQUADRON

Operated: formed 28 August 1940 at Blackpool, disbanded 6 January 1947 at RAF Coltishall.

Code letters: UZ

Aircraft: Hurricane, Spitfire, Mustang

Bases: Church Fenton from 4 September 1940, Ternhill from 7 November 1940, Northolt from 2 April 1941, Speke from 7 October 1941, Church Stanton from 12 December 1941, Kirton-in-Lindsay from 3 May 1942, Northolt from 15 June 1942, Croydon from 30 June 1942, Northolt from 7 July 1942, Hutton Cranswick from 11 March 1943, Catterick from 30 May 1943, Gravesend from 11 August 1943, Friston from 18 August 1943, Heston from 21 September 1943, Llanbedr from 19 December 1943, Heston from 1 January 1944, Llanbedr from 15 March 1944, Heston from 20 March 1944, Coolham from 1 April 1944, Holmsley South from 22 June 1944, Ford from 25 June 1944, Brenzett from 7 July 1944, Andrews Field from 10 October 1944, Coltishall from 10 August 1945, Fairwood Common from 8 October 1945, Coltishall from 18 November 1945.

Total score: 70 enemy aircraft destroyed, 16½ probably destroyed and over 28 damaged[8] as well as over 57 flying bombs V1.

Losses (killed in operations and training): 35

Commanding Officers: Sqn Ldr Tadeusz Rolski from 20 August 1940, Sqn Ldr Jerzy Orzechowski from 23 October 1940, Sqn Ldr Tadeusz Rolski from 25 October 1940, Sqn Ldr Jerzy Zaremba from 27 June 1941 (†), Sqn Ldr Jerzy Słoński-Ostoja from 15 August 1941 (†), Sqn Ldr Antoni Wczelik from 30 August 1941 (†), Sqn Ldr Tadeusz Czerwiński from 14 April 1942 (†), Sqn Ldr Kazimierz Rutkowski from 23 August 1942, Sqn Ldr Włodzimierz Karwowski from 17 March 1943, Sqn Ldr Stanisław Łapka from 1 January 1944 (SEC), Sqn Ldr Janusz Marciniak from 7 June 1944 (†), Sqn Ldr Paweł Niemiec from 27 June 1944, Sqn Ldr Józef Żulikowski from 25 September 1944, Sqn Ldr Józef Jeka from 25 May 1945, Sqn Ldr Tadeusz Andersz from 4 May 1946.

RAF Commanders: Sqn Ldr Douglas R. Scott from 4 September 1940, Sqn Ldr Denys E. Gillam from 1 December 1940 to 3 March 1941.

NO. 307 'CITY OF LWÓW.[9] LWÓW EAGLE OWLS SQUADRON (NIGHT FIGHTER)

Operated: formed 24 August 1940 at Blackpool, disbanded 2 January 1947 at RAF Coltishall.

Code letters: EW

Aircraft: Defiant, Beaufighter, Mosquito

Bases: Kirton-in-Lindsey from 5 September 1940, Jurby from November 7, 1940 (including operating from Squires Gate), Squires Gate from 27 January 1941, Colerne from 26 March 1941, Exeter from 26 April 1941 (including operating from Pembrey), Fairwood Common from 15 April 1943 (including operating from Predennack), Predennack from 7 August 1943, Drem from 9 November 1943, Coleby Grange from 2 March 1944, Church Fenton from 4 May 1944, Castle Camps from 28 January 1945, Coltishall from 18 May 1945, Horsham St. Faith from 24 August 1945.

Total score: 30¾ enemy aircraft destroyed, 7 probably destroyed and over 17 damaged.[10]

Losses (killed in operations and training): 47 + 2 after the war

Commanding Officers: Flt Lt Stanisław Pietraszkiewicz from 28 August 1940, Sqn Ldr Kazimierz Benz from 14 October 1940, Sqn Ldr Stanisław Grodzicki from 14 November 1940 (K),[11] Wg Cdr Jerzy Antonowicz from 11 June 1941 (†), Sqn Ldr Maksymilian Lewandowski from 24 October 1941, Wg Cdr Stanisław Brejnak from 16 November 1941, Wg Cdr Jan Michałowski from 23 July 1942 (†), Sqn Ldr Gerard Ranoszek from 22 March 1943, Wg Cdr Jerzy Orzechowski from 1 April 1943, Wg Cdr Maksymilian Lewandowski from 8 November 1943, Wg Cdr Gerard Ranoszek from 21 May 1944, Wg Cdr Stanisław Andrzejewski from 21 December 1944, Wg Cdr Jerzy Damsz from 1 February 1946.

RAF Commander: Sqn Ldr George C. Tomlinson from 5 September 1940 to 18 March 1941.

NO. 308 'CITY OF CRACOW' SQUADRON

Operated: formed 9 September 1940 at Blackpool, disbanded 12 December 1946 at RAF Coltishall.

Code letters: ZF

Aircraft: Hurricane, Spitfire

Bases: Speke from 12 September 1940; Baginton from 25 September 1940; Chilbolton from 1 June 1941; Northolt from 26 June 1941; Woodvale from 12 December 1941; Exeter from 1 April 1942; Hutton Cranswick from 7 May 1942, Redhill from 30 June 1942; Hutton Cranswick from 7 July 1942; Heston from 30 July 1942; Ipswich from 1 September 1942; Heston from 21 September 1942; Northolt from 21 October 1942; Church Fenton from 29 April 1943; Friston from 7 September 1943; Heston from 21 September 1943; Northolt from 11 November 1943; Hutton Cranswick from 2 December 1943; Northolt from 18 December 1943; Llanbedr from 8 March 1944; Northolt from 15 March 1944; Deanland from 1 April 1944; Chailey from 26 April 1944; Appledram from 28 June 1944; Ford from 16 July 1944; Plumetôt B. 10 from 3 August 1944; Fresnoy Folny/Londiniere B.31 from 5 September 1944; Lille/Vendeville B.51 from 10 September 1944; Antwerp/Deurne B.70 from 3 October 1944; St. Denijs Westrem B.61 from 11 October 1944; Grimbergen B.60 from 13 January 1945; Gilze-Rijen B.77 from 8 March 1945; Nordhorn B.101 from 13 April 1945; Fairwood Common from 28 April 1945; Varrelbusch B.113 from 2 June 1945; Ahlhorn B.111 from 14 September 1945; Hethel from 7 October 1946.

Total score: 69½ enemy aircraft destroyed, 13 probably destroyed and 21 damaged

Losses (killed in operations and training): 36

Commanding Officers: Sqn Ldr Stefan Łaszkiewicz from 9 September 1940; Sqn Ldr Walerian Jasionowski from 10 November 1940; Sqn Jerzy Orzechowski from 8 December 1940; Sqn Ldr Marian Pisarek from 23 June 1941 (K); Sqn Ldr Marian Wesołowski from 10 December 1941 (†); Sqn Ldr Tadeusz Nowierski from 9 January 1942; Sqn Ldr Feliks Szyszka from 6 May 1942 (†); Sqn Ldr Walerian Żak from 17 May 1942; Sqn Ldr Franciszek Kornicki 12 February 1943; Sqn Ldr Paweł Niemiec from 3 March 1943; Sqn Ldr Józef Żulikowski from 18 May 1943; Sqn Ldr Witold Retinger from 20 March 1944; Sqn Ldr Karol Pniak from 11 November 1944; Sqn Ldr Ignacy Olszewski from 1 July 1945; Sqn Ldr Karol Pniak from September 1946.

RAF Commanders: Sqn Ldr John A. Davis from 18 September 1940 (†); Sqn Ldr Brenus G. Morris from 17 October 1940 to 7 February 1941

NO. 315 'CITY OF DĘBLIN' SQUADRON

Operated: formed 21 January 1941 at RAF Acklington, disbanded 14 January 1947 at RAF Coltishall.

Code letters: PK

Aircraft: Hurricane, Spitfire, Mustang

Bases: Acklington from 21 January 1941; Speke from 13 March 1941; Northolt from 13 July 1941; Woodvale from 1 April 1942; Northolt from 5 September 1942; Hutton Cranswick from 1 June 1943; Ballyhalbert from 5 July 1943; Heston from 13 November 1943; Llanbedr from 19 December 1943; Heston from 1 January 1944; Llanbedr from 24 March 1944; Heston from 28 March 1944; Coolham from 1 April 1944; Ford (including short stay in Holmsley South) from 26 June 1944; Brenzett from 10 July 1944; Andrews Field from 10 October 1944; Coltishall from 24 October 1944; Peterhead from 30 October 1944; Andrews Field from 16 January 1945; Coltishall from 9 August 1945; Fairwood Common from 19 November 1945; Coltishall from 20 December 1945

Total score: 86 enemy aircraft destroyed, 18 probably destroyed and 28 damaged

Losses (killed in operations and training): 42 + 1 after the war

Commanding Officers: Sqn Ldr Stanisław Pietraszkiewicz from 21 January 1941 (PoW); Sqn Ldr Władysław Szcześniewski from 22 September 1941 (PoW); Sqn Ldr Stefan Janus from 12 November 1941; Sqn Ldr Mieczysław Wiórkiewicz from 6 May 1942; Sqn Ldr Tadeusz Sawicz from 25 September 1942; Sqn Ldr Jerzy Popławski from 16 April 1943; Sqn Ldr Eugeniusz Horbaczewski from 16 February 1944 (†); Sqn Ldr Tadeusz Andersz from 19 August 1944; Sqn Ldr Władysław Potocki from 6 April 1945; Sqn Ldr Jan Siekierski from 15 February 1946

RAF Commander: Sqn Ldr Humphrey D. Cooke from 25 January 1941 to 7 July 1941

NO. 316 'CITY OF WARSAW' SQUADRON[12]

Operated: formed 23 February 1941 at RAF Pembrey, disbanded 11 December 1946 at RAF Hethel.

Code letters: SZ

Aircraft: Hurricane, Spitfire, Mustang

Bases: Pembrey from 23 February 1941; Colerne from 18 June 1941; Church Stanton from 2 August 1941; Northolt from 12 December 1941; Heston from 22 April 1942; Croydon from 30 June 1942; Heston from 7 July 1942; Hutton Cranswick from 30 July 1942; Northolt from 11 March 1943; Acklington from 22 September 1943; Woodvale from 15 February 1944; Coltishall from 25 April 1944; West Malling from 1 July 1944; Friston from 11 July 1944; Coltishall from 27 August 1944; Andrews Field from 24 October 1944; Coltishall from 16 May 1945; Andrews Field from 10 August 1945; Wick from 28 November 1945; Hethel from 15 March 1946

Total score: 45½ enemy aircraft destroyed, 19 probably destroyed and 21 damaged; also over 68 V1 flying bombs

Losses (killed in operations and training): 38 + 2 after the war

Commanding Officers: Sqn Ldr Juliusz Frey from 22 February 1941; Sqn Ldr Wacław Wilczewski from 10 August 1941 (PoW); Sqn Ldr Aleksander Gabszewicz from 14 November 1941; Sqn Ldr Janusz Żurakowski from 6 June 1942; Sqn Ldr Marian Trzebiński from 1 January 1943; Sqn Ldr Paweł Niemiec from 15 September 1943; Sqn Ldr Bohdan Arct from 26 June 1944 (PoW); Sqn Ldr Zygmunt Drybański from 6 September 1944; Sqn Ldr Michał Cwynar from 3 July 1945; Sqn Ldr Paweł Niemiec from 12 October 1945

RAF Commander: Sqn Ldr Cornelius J. Donovan from 2 March 1941 to 22 June 1941

NO. 317 'CITY OF WILNO'[13] SQUADRON

Operated: formed 22 February 1941 at RAF Acklington, disbanded 18 December 1946 at RAF Hethel.

Code letters: JH

Aircraft: Hurricane, Spitfire

Bases: Acklington from 22 February 1941; Ouston from 29 April 1941; Colerne from 26 June 1941; Fairwood Common from 27 June 1941; Exeter from 27 July 1941; Northolt from 1 April 1942; Croydon from 30 June 1942; Northolt from 7 July 1942; Woodvale from 5 September 1942; Kirton-in-Lindsey from 13 February 1943; Martlesham Heath from 29 April 1943; Heston from 1 June 1943; Perranporth from 21 June 1943; Fairlop from 21 August 1943; Northolt from 21 September 1943; Southend from 2 December 1943; Northolt from 18 December 1943; Deanland from 1 April 1944; Chailey from 26 April 1944; Appledram from 28 June 1944; Ford from 16 July 1944; Plumetôt B.10 from 3 August 1944; Fresnoy Folny/Londiniere B.31 from 5 September 1944; Lille/Vendeville B.51 from 10 September 1944; Antwerp/Deurne B.70 from 3 October 1944; St. Denijs Westrem B.61 from 11 October 1944; Grimbergen B. 60 from 13 January 1945; Gilze-Rijen B.75 from 8 March 1945; Nordhorn B.101 from 13 April 1945; Varrelbusch B. 113 from 30 April 1945; Ahlhorn B. 111 from 14 September 1945; Hethel from 7 October 1946

Total score: 48⅓ enemy aircraft destroyed, 10 probably destroyed and 26 damaged

Losses (killed in operations and training): 25[14]

Commanding Officers: Sqn Ldr Stanisław Brzezina from 20 February 1941; Sqn Ldr Henryk Szczęsny from 20 August 1941; Sqn Ldr Józef Brzeziński from 12 November 1941 (†); Sqn Ldr Piotr Ozyra from 16 March 1942 (†); Sqn Ldr Stanisław Skalski from 30 April 1942; Sqn Ldr Zbigniew Czaykowski from 9 November 1942; Sqn Ldr Zbigniew Wróblewski from 15 April 1943; Sqn Ldr Franciszek Kornicki from 6 May 1943; Sqn Ldr Włodzimierz Miksa from 1 January 1944; Sqn Ldr Władysław Gnyś from 27 August 1944 (SEC); Sqn Ldr Marian Chełmecki from 28 August 1944; Sqn Ldr Paweł Niemiec from 17 May 1945; Sqn Ldr Marian Trzebiński from 25 October 1945

RAF Commanders: Sqn Ldr Christopher J. Mount from 20 February 1941 to 25 April 1941; Sqn Ldr Alexander N. Cole from 25 April 1941 to 19 June 1941

Appendix III

Losses of Polish Fighter Personnel in RAF and USAAF Squadrons (Killed in Action and Training)

No. 3 Sqn RAF: 3; No. 19 Sqn RAF: 1; No. 23 Sqn RAF: 1; No. 25 Sqn RAF: 1; No. 32 Sqn RAF: 2; No. 41 Sqn RAF: 1; No. 54 Sqn RAF: 1; No. 56 Sqn RAF: 1; 61st FS USAAF: 1; No. 65 Sqn RAF: 2; No. 72 Sqn RAF: 1; No. 79 Sqn RAF: 1; No. 87 Sqn RAF: 1; No. 92 Sqn RAF: 1; No. 111 Sqn RAF: 2; No. 112 Sqn RAF: 2; No. 145 Sqn RAF: 4; No. 151 Sqn RAF: 2; No. 152 Sqn RAF: 2; No. 183 Sqn RAF: 1; No. 213 Sqn RAF: 2; No. 219 Sqn RAF: 1; No. 222 Sqn RAF: 1; No. 238 Sqn RAF: 2; No. 241 Sqn RAF: 2; No. 245 Sqn RAF: 1; No. 253 Sqn RAF: 1; No. 310 (Cz) Sqn RAF: 1; No. 401 Sqn RCAF: 1; No. 241 Sqn RAF: 2; No. 501 Sqn RAF: 3; No. 540 Sqn RAF: 1; No. 601 Sqn RAF: 1; No. 602 Sqn RAF: 2; No. 605 Sqn RAF: 4; No. 607 Sqn RAF: 1; No. 610 Sqn RAF: 1; No. 615 Sqn RAF: 1

Appendix IV

Scores of Top Twenty Polish Pilots during French Campaign 1940

Cpl. Eugeniusz Nowakiewicz 3⅚ – 0 – 0[1]; Sub. Lt, Stanisław Chałupa 2⅔ – 0 – 0;
Sub. Lt Wacław Król 2 – 1 – 0; Sub. Lt. Jerzy Czerniak 2 – 0 – 0 (K); Lt. Tadeusz
Czerwiński 2 – 0 – 0 (K); Sgt Leopold Flanek 2 – 0 – 0 (K); Sub. Lt. Erwin Kawnik
2 – 0 – 0 (K); Sub. Lt. Aleksy Żukowski 2 – 0 – 0 (K); Lt. Arsen Cebrzyński 1⅚ – 0 – 0
(K); Maj. Mieczysław Mümler 1½ – 0 – 0; Sub. Lt. Marian Trzebiński 1½ – 0 – 0; Plt.
Com. Antoni Beda 1⅓ – 0 – 0; Cpt. Antoni Wczelik 1⅓ – 0 – 0 (K); Sub. Lt. Czesław
Główczyński 1 – 1 – 0; Sub. Lt. Władysław Gnyś 1 – 0 – 1; Sub. Lt. Władysław Chciuk
1 – 0 – 0; Sub. Lt. Jan Daszewski 1 – 0 – 0 (K); Lt. Aleksander Gabszewicz 1 – 0 – 0; Sub.
Lt. Rajmund Kalpas 1 – 0 – 0; Sub. Lt. Włodzimierz Karwowski 1 – 0 – 0.

Appendix V

Scores of Top Twenty Polish Pilots during the Battle of Britain

Flg Off/Acting Sqn Ldr Witold Urbanowicz 15 – 1 – 0; Sgt Antoni Głowacki 8 – 1 – 3; Flg Off Zdzisław Henneberg 8 – 1 – 1 (K); Plt Off Jan Zumbach 8 – 1 – 0; Sgt Eugeniusz Szaposznikow 8 – 0 – 1; Sgt Józef Jeka 7½ – 0 – 3; Plt Off Mirosław Ferić 7 – 1 – 0 (K); Sgt Marian Bełc 6 – 0 – 0 (K); Sgt Stanisław Karubin 6 – 0 – 0 (K); Flg Off Ludwik Paszkiewicz 6 – 0 – 0 (K); Plt Off Bolesław Własnowolski 5 – 0 – 0 (K); Plt Off Stanisław Skalski 4⅔ – 0 – 2; Flg Off Karol Pniak 4½ – 2 – 1½ ; Flg Off Stefan Witorzeńć 4½ – 0 – 2; Plt Off Witold Łokuciewski 4 – 1 – 0; Flg Off Marian Pisarek 4 – 0 – 1 (K); Sgt Mirosław Wojciechowski 3½ – 0 – 0; Flg Off Tadeusz Nowierski 3 – 1 – 3; Plt Off Tadeusz Nowak 3 – 1 – 1 (K); Plt Off Janusz Żurakowski 3 – ½ – 0.

Appendix VI

Polish Air Force Aces and their Scores Claimed under RAF and USAAF Command

Wg Cdr Witold Urbanowicz 17 − 1 − 0; Sgt Josef František 17 − 1 − 0,[1] Sqn Ldr Eugeniusz Horbaczewski 16½ − 1 − 1 (K); Wg Cdr Stanisław Skalski 14⅔ − 2 − 4; Flt Lt Bolesław Gładych 14 − 2 − ½ (+ 4 not approved by HQ PAF and 1 claimed as aerial victory yet approved as destroyed on the ground);[2] Wg Cdr Jan Zumbach 12⅓ − 5 − 1; Plt Off Michał Maciejowski 10½ − 1 − 1; Wg Cdr Marian Pisarek 9½ − 1 -1 (K); Wt Off Aleksander Chudek 9 − 1 − 1 (K); Wg Cdr Jan Falkowski 9 − 1 − 0; Flt Lt Stanisław Brzeski 8½ − 2 − 1; Sqn Ldr Antoni Głowacki 8⅓ − 3 − 4; Gp Cpt Aleksander Gabszewicz 8 − 1⅓ − 3; Flt Lt Mirosław Ferić 8 − 1 − 1 (K); Sqn Ldr Zdzisław Henneberg 8 − 1 − 1 (K); Flt Lt Eugeniusz Szaposznikow 8 − 0 − 1; Sqn Ldr Henryk Szczęsny 7⅓ − 0 − 1; Sqn Ldr Henryk Pietrzak 7½ − 1 − 1; Sqn Ldr Józef Jeka 7½ − 0 − 3; Flt Lt Adolf Pietrasiak 7½ − 0 − 0 (K); Sqn Ldr Witold Łokuciewski 7 − 3 − 0; Sqn Ldr Bolesław Drobiński 7 − 1⅓ − 0; Wg Cdr Stefan Janus 6 − 0 − 1; Wg Cdr Wacław Król 6 − 0 − ⅓; Plt Off Marian Bełc 6 − 0 − 0 (K); Sgt Stanisław Karubin 6 − 0 − 0 (K); Flt Lt Ludwik Paszkiewicz 6 − 0 − 0 (K); Wg Cdr Kazimierz Rutkowski 5½ − 2 − 1; Gp Cpt Stefan Witorzeńć 5½ − 0 − 2; Flg Off Franciszek Surma 5 − 3⅓ − 1 (K); Flt Lt Stanisław Blok 5 − 1 − 3; Flt Lt Kazimierz Sporny 5 − 1 − 1; Flg Off Mieczysław Adamek 5 − 1 − 0 (K); Flt Lt Grzegorz Sołogub 5 − 1 − 0; Wt Off Jakub Bargiełowski 5 − 0 − 3; Sqn Ldr Jerzy Popławski 5 − 0 − 2; Sqn Ldr Wacław Łapkowski 5 − 0 − 1 (K); Flg Off Bolesław Własnowolski 5 − 0 − 0 (K).

Polish Air Force Aces and their Sumaric Scores 1939–1945

Wg Cdr Stanisław Skalski $18\frac{11}{12}$ – 2 – $4\frac{1}{3}$ (P: $4\frac{1}{4}$ – 0 – $1\frac{1}{3}$);[1] Wg Cdr Witold Urbanowicz 17 – 1 – 0; Sgt Josef František 17 – 1 – 0; Sqn Ldr Eugeniusz Horbaczewski $16\frac{1}{2}$ – 1 – 1 (K); Flt Lt Bolesław Gładych 14 – 2 – $\frac{1}{2}$ (+ 4 not approved by HQ PAF and 1 claimed as aerial victory yet approved as destroyed on the ground); Wg Cdr Jan Zumbach $12\frac{1}{3}$ – 5 – 1; Wg Cdr Marian Pisarek 12 – 1 – 2 (P: $3\frac{1}{2}$ – 0 – 1)(K); Plt Off Michał Maciejowski $10\frac{1}{2}$ – 1 – 1; Gp Cpt Aleksander Gabszewicz $9\frac{1}{2}$ – $1\frac{1}{3}$ – 3 (P: $\frac{1}{2}$ – 0 – 0); Sqn Ldr Henryk Szczęsny $9\frac{1}{3}$ – 1 – 2 (P: 2 – 1 – 1); Flt Lt Mirosław Ferić $9\frac{1}{3}$ – 1 – 1 (P: $1\frac{1}{3}$ – 0 – 0)(K); Wt Off Aleksander Chudek 9 – 1 – 1 (K); Wg Cdr Jan Falkowski 9 – 1 – 0; Flt Lt Stanisław Brzeski $8\frac{1}{2}$ – 2 – 1; Sqn Ldr Zdzisław Henneberg $8\frac{1}{2}$ – 1 – 1 (F: $\frac{1}{2}$ – 0 – 0)(K); Wg Cdr Wacław Król $8\frac{1}{2}$ – 1 – $\frac{1}{3}$ (P: $\frac{1}{2}$ – 0 – 0; F: 2 – 1 – 0); Sqn Ldr Antoni Głowacki $8\frac{1}{3}$ – 3 – 4; Flt Lt Eugeniusz Szaposznikow $8\frac{1}{3}$ – 0 – 1 (F: $\frac{1}{3}$ – 0 – 0); Flt Lt Adolf Pietrasiak $8\frac{1}{10}$ – 0 – $\frac{2}{5}$ (F: $\frac{3}{5}$ – 0 – $\frac{2}{5}$) (K); Sqn Ldr Witold Łokuciewski 8 – $3\frac{1}{2}$ – 0 (P: – $\frac{1}{2}$ – 0; F: 1 – 0 – 0); Sqn Ldr Henryk Pietrzak $7\frac{1}{2}$ – 1 – 1; Sqn Ldr Józef Jeka $7\frac{1}{2}$ – 0 – 3; Sqn Ldr Bolesław Drobiński 7 – $1\frac{1}{3}$ – 0; Plt Off Marian Bełc 7 – 0 – 0 (P: 1 – 0 – 0)(K); Sgt Stanisław Karubin 7 – 0 – 0 (P: 1 – 0 – 0) (K); Sqn Ldr Karol Pniak $6\frac{3}{4}$ – 2 – $2\frac{5}{6}$ (P: $2\frac{1}{4}$ – 0 – $\frac{1}{3}$); Sqn Ldr Wacław Łapkowski $6\frac{1}{3}$ – 0 – 1 (P: $1\frac{1}{3}$ – 0 – 0) (K); Wg Cdr Stefan Janus 6 – 0 – 1; Flt Lt Ludwik Paszkiewicz 6 – 0 – 0 (K); Wg Cdr Kazimierz Rutkowski $5\frac{1}{2}$ – 2 – 1; Sqn Ldr Czesław Główczyński $5\frac{1}{2}$ – 2 – 1 (P: $3\frac{1}{2}$ – 0 – 1; F: 1 – 2 – 0); Sqn Ldr Michał Cwynar $5\frac{1}{2}$ – 1 – 0 (P: $4\frac{1}{2}$ – 0 – 0); Gp Cpt Stefan Witorzeń $5\frac{1}{2}$ – 0 – 2; Gp Cpt Mieczysław Mümler $5\frac{1}{2}$ – 0 – $1\frac{1}{2}$ (P: 3 – 0 – 0; F: $1\frac{1}{2}$ – 0 – 0); Flg Off Bolesław Własnowolski $5\frac{1}{2}$ – 0 – 0 (P: $\frac{1}{2}$ – 0 – 0) (K); Flg Off Mieczysław Adamek $5\frac{9}{20}$ – 1 – 0 (P: $\frac{9}{20}$ – 0 – 0)(K); Flg Off Franciszek Surma 5 – $3\frac{1}{3}$ – 1 (K); Flt Lt Stanisław Blok 5 – 1 – 3; Flt Lt Kazimierz Sporny 5 – 1 – 1; Flt Lt Grzegorz Sołogub 5 – 1 – 0; Wt Off Jakub Bargiełowski 5 – 0 – 3; Sqn Ldr Jerzy Popławski 5 – 0 – 2; Plt Off Eugeniusz Nowakiewicz $4\frac{5}{6}$[2] – 1 – 1 F: $3\frac{5}{6}$ – 0 – $\frac{1}{2}$); Sqn Ldr Władysław Potocki $4\frac{3}{4}$ – 0 – 1; Flt Lt Kazimierz Wünsche $4\frac{1}{2}$ – 1 – 0; Flg Off Tadeusz Nowak $4\frac{1}{2}$ – 1 – 1 (P: $\frac{1}{2}$ – 0 – 0) (K); Flg Off Kazimierz Sztramko $4\frac{1}{3}$ – 0 – 0 (F: 1 – 0 – 0); Wt Off Mirosław Wojciechowski $4\frac{1}{2}$ – 0 – 0; Plt Off Jan Kremski $4\frac{14}{15}$ – $\frac{1}{3}$ – $1\frac{1}{15}$ (P: 2 – 0 – 0 (K); F: ; Sqn Ldr Tadeusz Koc $4\frac{1}{3}$ – 3 – 0; Wt Off Mieczysław Popek 4 (3 + 2 shared) – 0 – 2 (K); Flt Lt Stanisław Chałupa $3\frac{2}{3}$ (3 + 2 shared) – 2 – 0; Sqn Ldr Marian Wesołowski $2\frac{14}{15}$ (2 + 4 shared) – 0 – $2\frac{1}{15}$ (K); Flt Lt Bronisław Kosiński $2\frac{3}{5}$ (2 + 3 shared) – 0 – $\frac{2}{5}$ (K); Flt Lt Jerzy Radomski $3\frac{1}{3}$ (2 + 3 shared) – $\frac{1}{3}$ – 4; Sqn Ldr Władysław Gnyś 3 (2 + 3 shared) – 0 – 1

Photos courtesy of: the late Stefan Andersz, the late Bohdan Arct, Peter Arnold, Association of the 4th Fighter Group, Mark Baczkiewicz, the late Jakub Bargiełowski, Befinger family, Dr Bartłomiej Belcarz, Bieniek family, the late Stanisław Birtus, the late Stanisław Bochniak, Bondarczuk family, Melvin Brownless, Andrzej Brzezina, Brzózkiewicz family, Cedrowski family, Celak family, Grzegorz Cieliszak, the late Stanisław Chałupa, Jack Cook, the late Michał Cwynar, the late Jerzy B. Cynk, Damsz family, the late Józef Derma, Tomasz Drecki, Brendan Finucane QC, Stefan Gabszewicz, the late Bolesław Gładych, the late Antoni Głowacki, the late Jerzy Główczewski, the late Czesław Główczyński, Steve Gorzula, Łukasz Gredys, Robert Gretzyngier, Jaeschke family, the late Marian Jankiewicz, Jaszczak family, the late Edward Jaworski, the late Jan Kawa, Kobierzycki family, the late Tadeusz Koc, the late Wojciech Kołaczkowski, the late Franciszek Kornicki, the late Mieczysław Kowalski, the late Zdzisław Krasnodębski, the late Józef Krzywonos, Lech Laszkiewicz, Lesław Latawiec, Zbigniew Legierski, the Littlefriends website courtesy of Peter Randall, Łapka family, the late Bronisław Mach, the late Jan Maliński, the late Stanisław Marcisz, Wojtek Matusiak, Tim McCann, the late Jerzy Mencel, Mierzejewski family, Nick Najbicz, Neyder family, Dorota Nowakowska for Łapkowski family, the late Bożydar Nowosielski-Ślepowron, Karol Paprocki, Polish Aviation Museum Cracow, Richard Popek, the late Jerzy Popławski, the late Jan Preihs, the late Alfred Price via Wojtek Matusiak, the late Henryk Pietrzak, Prusak family, Peter Randall, Wilhelm Ratuszyński, Marek Rogusz, Daniel Rolski, the late Stefan Ryll, the late Mieczysław Sawicki, Sawoszczyk family, the late Stanisław Skalski, the late Piotr Skrzypczak, the late Stanisław Socha, Paul Sołogub, Sam Sox, the late Wacław Stański, Dr Grzegorz Śliżewski, the late Czesław Tarkowski, the late Franciszek Tomczak, the late Zdzisław Uchwat, the late Jan Wawrzyczny via Zbigniew Legierski, the late Wacław Włodarczyk, the late Władysław Zając, Wojciech Zmyślony

Very special thanks to Steve Brooking, Rodney Byles (for keeping me in order), Robert Gretzyngier, Wojtek Matusiak, Peter Randall and, as always, to my beloved wife and friend Marzena.

Notes

Introduction

1. Gp Cpt T.N. McEvoy, Secret. The Polish Fighter Pilot.
2. In free Poland he commanded various air force schools and the 4th Air Regiment
3. Over 80 per cent of the initial number of men available prior to the outbreak of the Second World War. Later even some of the captured ones, managed to escape the Germans and Soviets, crossing Tatra Mountains and travelling to France and onto Great Britain. 332 Polish airmen (including fighter pilots) were murdered by the Soviets or died in Russian captivity. The lucky ones left USSR with General Władysław Anders army after the Gen. Władysław Sikorski – Ivan Mayski agreement.
4. Including 10 shared with the French pilots
5. Different authors suggest numbers that differ, from 52 to 32 E/A destroyed only by the Polish pilots
6. 25 October 1939
7. At that time the R/T equipment fitted to British aircraft was of much poorer quality, than in later years, causing lot of incovenience for their own pilots, therefore it was rightfully assumed that the foreigners wouldn't be able to use it at all as they would not understand the orders.
8. Claiming shared destruction of a He 111
9. His first non-operational sortie in 145 Sqn took place on 18 July 1940
10. Two books by this author were published covering Polish participation in the Battle of Britain: *The Polish Few. Polish Airmen in the Battle of Britain*, Pen & Sword, Barnsley 2018; *Poles in the Battle of Britain. A photographic album of the Polish Few*, Pen & Sword, Barnsley 2020, where operations carried out by the Polish pilots were described in details.
11. Polish participation in the Battle of Britain is often associated with No. 303 Sqn only, although Polish fighter pilots attached to RAF squdrons fought as early as in first phase of the Battle.
12. A lone commander of RAF Coltishall in Britain as well as Varrelbusch B.113 and Ahlhorn B.111 in occupied Germany. There were also Polish Station Commanders of RAF Northolt: Gp Cpt Mieczysław Mümler (ironically at some point RAF Northolt was known as the Polish Station where 'English was also spoken'); RAF Heston: Wg Cdrs Stanisław Brzezina and Zdzisław Krasnodębski; and RAF Coltishall, Andrews Field; Wick and Hethel respectively: Wg Cdr Julian Kowalski. In fact their roles were deputy base commanders with the RAF commander having a superior role.

13. Poland regained its independence from Soviet rule in 1989. By then many of the ex-airmen had passed away or were living their final years far away from their homeland.
14. As well as other PAF squadrons, which are often erroneously called 'RAF squadrons'. The Polish – British agreement signed on August 5, 1940 stated that: 'Polish Armed Forces (comprising Land, Sea and Air Forces) shall be organised and employed under British Command in its character as the Allied High Command, as the Armed Forces of the Republic of Poland allied with the United Kingdom.' Purposely or not, calling Polish manned squadrons 'RAF Squadrons' downgrades the role that the Polish Allies played and fully deserved.
15. Witold Urbanowicz. His colleague Stanisław Skalski asked for permission to fight as well, but before the official decision had been made, the war with Japan had ended. There were also unofficial 'plans' to send Polish squadrons (most certainly bombers) and glider experts to support Kuomintang military forces of China in 1942. These 'plans' or rather impractical promises made by Gen. Sikorski, were unrealistic and never materialised.
16. Formed on 1 April 1941
17. Formed on 18 August 1941
18. Established in 1941
19. The late Jerzy B. Cynk, a well-known Polish historian, suggested a total number of 107 E/A including four Soviet planes.
20. These numbers do not include fighter crews killed in flying accidents after the war.
21. This number does not include Polish fighter pilots posted for operational duties to bomber squadrons (e.g. Cpt Tadeusz Opulski, former commander of 112th Fighter Squadron in Poland and Fighter Section in France, killed while in No. 18 OTU) or for training duties to flying schools or being under training
22. Two Dornier Do 17s that he claimed are the first aerial victories of the Second World War. His commander Cpt Mieczysław Medwecki was the first Allied airman killed in the Second World War.

Chapter 2
1. The tail unit of this aircraft can be seen to this day in Musee du Sopuvenir at Haut-le-Wastia, Belgium
2. Also Miles Magister and No. 103 Sqn's Fairey Battle, both from RAF as well as unknown MS. 406

Chapter 3
1. Even now numerous publications claim that the Poles came to Britain to (finally) fly modern aircraft, failing to mention that in mid 1930s the Air Ministry suffered from a similar problem as the pre-war Polish Military Aviation (not to mention that Poland was recently a re-born country, after 123 years of non existence; while the British Empire ruled almost half of the world): the lack of modern fighter aircraft and only in February 1936 the plan of introducing new types was finally approved.

The RAF introduced Hawker Hurricanes at the end of 1937 and Supermarine Spitfires in the second half of 1938, both initially designed as anti-bombers, that resulted in both not being fitted with cannon until 1941 (see Polish PZL P.24). Very little is mentioned that in many cases Polish pilots had more experience than their British instructors, including combat experience. Also a language barrier is mentioned as a Polish Achille's heel of 1940. A large percentage of Polish airmen fluently spoke French, plus languages of neighbouring countries: German, Russian etc, while English was known only to very few of them, not being an international language at that time, hence not considered to be needed before the war (not only in Poland).

2. Also Sgt Josef František, who died in a flying accident, and Sgt Antoni Siudak killed by a bomb while in a Hurricane on the ground at RAF Northolt.

Chapter 4
1. After No. 300 Bomber Squadron
2. Nine out of seventeen pilots of the initial group posted to No. 302 flew with GC 1/145, four with the other GCs
3. Beda (GC I/2) and Gnyś (GC III/1), both No. 302 Sqn; Duryasz No. 213 Sqn RAF. Gnyś also flew in combat in Poland (121st Fighter Squadron) claiming the first aerial victories of the Second World War, meanwhile Duryasz flew operationally with so called 'Instructors' Flight', defending Dęblin area
4. No. 302 Sqn Operations Record Book
5. Bf 109 F-2 Werk Nr 5647 black '3' from 1./JG 3
6. No. 302 Sqn lost two other Hurricanes during this combat: Z2523 WX-G flown by Sgt Marian Domagała and Z3098 WX-A piloted by Sqn Ldr Piotr Łaguna; both survived.
7. One of two pilots with the same first and second name serving in No. 306 Sqn
8. Many Polish airmen used them until the end of the war, some others preferred to wear the Polish AF long leather coats. You can see them on many recently colourised photos in brown (!), thanks to the modern artists' ignorance!
9. Who recently returned to No. 303 Sqn after convalescence. He was wounded during the Battle of Britain.
10. Zumbach had dual citizenship; his mother was Polish
11. 7th Squadron is often said to have been 'formed by American volunteers', where in fact this unit was organised on 7 November 1918 in Kraków, initially as 3rd Aviation Squadron. 3rd Squadron fought during the Polish – Ukrainian war, being dispatched to Lwów. On 22 December 1918 the unit was renamed as 7th Aviation Squadron. In April of 1919 transformation process has started, with 7th Squadron becoming a fighter unit. First Fokker E.Vs arrived, followed by the order issued in May 1919 that was changing the squadron's designation (despite this unit still flew reconnaissance missions using various types of aircraft and kept its original name). In August 1919 7th Aviation Squadron received Albatros D.IIIs (in fact Oeffags, built in Austria under German licence). A group of American volunteer–pilots was

attached to 7th Squadron on 17 October 1919 and soon after the unit was renamed as 7th Combat Squadron 'Kościuszko'. This way Americans wanted to pay tribute to the Polish national hero, who also fought for American independence. Then on 31 December 1919 the unit was once more renamed as 7th Polish – American 'Kościuszko' Fighter Unit. Demobilised American pilots left on 10 May 1921 whilst the squadron continued its history and changing its number.

12. Cooper became a well-known film producer ('King Kong' 1933); during the Second World War he was an initiator of what was later known as 'Flying Tigers' Squadron, operating in China against the Japanese. Witold Urbanowicz, the former commander of No. 303 Sqn, also flew with this squadron.

13. By 23rd Tactical Air Base. In 2007 'Kościuszko' badge was also taken into space by two members (Americans of Polish roots) of Discovery Space Shuttle.

14. Łapkowski, who was the natural choice to assume command of No. 303 Sqn, was wounded and admitted to hospital, Strzembosz returned to Northolt three days later. Both Spitfires were damaged.

15. Czechoslovak pilot serving in PAF

16. The earliest photo of No. 303 aircraft adorned with PAF marking was taken on 20 January 1942. The only exemptions were Hawker Hurricanes received from No. 302 Squadron during the Battle of Britain, so far however photos of a single Hurricane P3939 confirm it.

17. Yet Kołaczkowski's first name 'Wojtek' remained.

18. 23 September 1943

19. Precisely it was 8⅝

20. Including Belgian, British, Canadian, Czechoslovak, New Zealand, Norwegian and USAAF squadrons! The second squadron on top scorers' list was also Polish, No. 317 'City of Wilno' with 8⅓ E/A destroyed. Sqn Ldr Tadeusz Nowierski from No. 1 Polish Wing claimed 2 E/A damaged.

21. In rank of Sergeant, flying with No. 501 Sqn RAF

22. In Polish letter Q is rarely used and it is pronounced as 'ku' or 'cu'. The name 'QQWCA' therefore in Polish reads 'kukułka' (cuckoo).

23. 8 April 1941 is a day when the transition has started, Mk Is were gradually flown away.

24. Flg Off Wiesław Choms was another pilot killed during the same combat

25. Except No. 309 Sqn, which started converting from Army Cooperation when flying Mustang Is, then received Hurricane IVs and IICs,

26. Formed on 9 September 1940

27. Together with another 308 pilot Flg Off Witalis Nikonow

28. 1 – 0 – 1 and 3 – 0 – 0 respectively, all Bf 109s

29. Another Spitfire VB AD363 SZ-R was also hit and its pilot Plt Off Tadeusz Dobrut-Dobrucki baled out but did not survive.

30. No. 308 Squadron continued traditions of the 2nd Air Regiment's fighter units and used former 121st Fighter Squadron's emblem. Unlike the 121st FS, the 308 Sqn's

badge had a black background that symbolised grief for the lost homeland instead of the original blue. In 1945 the arrow was pointing towards the aircraft's tail.

31. As there was a few months gap between forming the last Polish squadron in 1940 (No. 309 AAC on 7 October 1940) and approval of further PAF squadrons to be organised, numbers from batch 310 to 313 were allocated to: Nos. 310, 312 and 313 (all three fighter), 311 (bomber) Czechoslovak Squadrons RAF, with no. 314 not being allocated to any operational squadron.

32. No. 302 'City of Poznań' Sqn was named after fighter units of the 3rd Air Regiment at Poznań (Ławica airfield); Nos. 303 and 316 'City of Warsaw' Sqn were named after fighter units of the 1st Air Regiment at Warsaw (Okęcie airfield); No. 306 'City of Toruń' Sqn was named after fighter units of the 4th Air Regiment in Toruń and No. 308 'City of Cracow' was named after fighter units of the 2nd Air Regiment at Cracow (Rakowice airfield). There were quite complicated exceptions too, such as No. 307 'City of Lwów' that continued traditions of the 5th Air Regiment in Wilno, actually at Lida (Porubanek airfield) and of the 6th Air Regiment at Lwów (Skniłów airfield); No. 309 'Czerwieńska Province' Sqn was named after Cherven Cities claimed by Poland since X Century and continued traditions of the 6th Air Regiment at Lwów (Skniłów airfield). No. 317 'City of Wilno' Sqn was named after Polish town of Wilno, but was continuing traditions of fighter units from the 5th Air Regiment in Wilno, at Lida (Porubanek airfield) and of the 6th Air Regiment at Lwów (Skniłów); and No. 318 'City of Gdańsk' Sqn was named after free city of Gdańsk as there was no air regiment stationed in a city claimed by Poland and Germany (the nearest base was Naval Air Arm Base at Puck, Pucka Bay).

33. There are pictures known that document application of a salamander emblem on 112th Fighter Squadron aircraft during the Polish Campaign 1939.

34. As Virginia Cherrill playing a blind flower girl

35. During the summer of 1941 No. 315 Sqn was equipped with both versions and almost all IIAs had their IIB equivalent with the same code!

36. From No. 412 Sqn RCAF

37. Pieces of EN856 are kept at Manx Aviation and Military Museum, Castletown, Isle of Man

38. Used during Polish Campaign 1939, previously 112th Fighter Squadron aircraft were marked with the fighting cockerel emblem. In case of No. 303 Sqn there is no evidence of using salamanders to decorate B Flight aircraft so far.

39. No. 317 Sqn received Spitfire Vs on 13 October and No. 302 Sqn on 30 October, 1941.

Chapter 5

1. Strasburger was killed on 25 October, 1942 when RAF Hospital Torquay was bombed

2. The bullet is still in the family collection

3. There were other Polish pilots flying in RAF and RCAF squadrons and participating in the Combined 'Dieppe Operation': Flg Off Edward Witke of No. 87 Sqn; Plt Off Jan Mozołowski and Flg Off Jan Wiejski, both No. 403 Sqn.

Appendix I

1. It is also believed that one MS.406 was used by Polish GC1/145
2. Pilots were posted to GCI/8 and GCI/1 for training on MB.151s and MB.152s.

Appendix II

1. Polish Air Force badges were never approved by the British Air Ministry
2. Including 1 – 1 – 1 claimed by non-Polish pilots of the squadron.
3. Shot down, evaded captivity
4. RAF officers posted to co-command Polish squadrons for initial period only
5. Named after Polish General and national hero
6. Including 15 – 5 – 3 claimed by non-Polish pilots of the squadron.
7. Killed while commanding squadron
8. Including 0 – 0 – ⅓ claimed by non-Polish pilots of the squadron. On top of the total score 3 E/A destroyed and 3 damaged on the ground.
9. Before the Second World War this was a town in Poland, now Lviv in Ukraine
10. On top of that 3 E/A destroyed, 2 probably destroyed and 1 damaged on the ground.
11. Killed in action or in an accident when serving in PAF.
12. One of two Polish fighter squadrons and one of three PAF squadrons named after Polish capital. No. 301 'Pomerania Province' Special Duty/Transport received an additional name 'Warsaw Defenders' on 15 September 1944 after being heavily involved in supplying Polish Home Army and the Warsaw Uprising.
13. Wilno – town in pre-war Poland, now Vilnius, capital of Lithuania
14. No. 317 Squadron's Flt Lt Lesław Szczerbiński, K/A on 4 May 1945 was also the last Polish airman killed during the Second World War

Appendix IV

1. Destroyed – probably destroyed – damaged

Appendix VI

1. A Czechoslovak pilot serving with PAF (posthumously promoted to officer's rank)
2. All claimed while flying in USAAF

Appendix VII

1. Claims from Poland 1939 and from France 1940 in brackets
2. There are two schools that give a definition of an ace: one is that all the victories should be summed and provided as whole, the second is that the shared victories shall be treated separately

Index